Love and Life
Student Guide

Love and Life

A Christian Sexual Morality
Guide for Teens

by Coleen Kelly Mast

Revised Edition

IGNATIUS PRESS   SAN FRANCISCO

Nihil obstat: Very Rev. Joseph J. Tapella
                   Vicar General
                   Diocese of Joliet, Illinois

Imprimatur: + Most Rev. Joseph L. Imesch,
                   Diocese of Joliet
                   July 5, 2005

The *nihil obstat* and *imprimatur* are official declarations that a book or pamphlet is free of doctrinal or moral error. No implication is contained therein that those who have granted the *nihil obstat* and *imprimatur* agree with the contents, opinions, or statements expressed in that work.

Corbis p. 103; Corbis/Bettmann p. 58B; Corbis/Pablo Corral V p. 29; Corbis Home and Family Vol. 126 p. 38; Corbis Modern Teen Vol. 231 p. 11, 22, 25, 28, 39, 41, 45, 47, 48 49, 58T, 59, 60, 61, 63, 65, 68, 89, 91, 97; Getty/Ryan McVay p. 17; ImageState Photos by Donna Day p. 51, 57T, 73, 74, 85, 92, 100, 101, 105, 128, 129, 130; Istock Photo p. 77; PhotoDisc Friends and Family Vol. 121 p. 19, 27, 40, 42, 44, 57B, 102, 119, 122, 123, 125, 126, 127; PhotoDisc Life is Good p. 12, 46, 113, 118; PhotoEdit/Mark Richards p. 115

Cover photo by Donna Day/ImageState
Design and production by Hespenheide Design
Illustrated by Robert Greisen

Library of Congress Control Number 2003105169
Printed in the United States of America

Dedication

You are the future of family life.
You are the future of the joy of loving.
You are the future of making your life
  something beautiful for God . . .
    a pure love.
That you love a girl
  or that you love a boy
    is beautiful.
but don't spoil it,
    don't destroy it.
Keep it pure.
  Keep your heart virgin.
Keep your love virgin,
  so that on the day of your marriage
  you can give something beautiful to each other . . .
    the joy of a pure love.

—Blessed Mother Teresa to young people

CONTENTS

UNIT IV THE CALL TO SERVE CHRIST IN LOVE

A PLAN FOR OUR HAPPINESS

Adolescence is a wonderful, adventurous time of life. However, sometimes it can be filled with puzzling questions that appear to have no answers, and confusing feelings that seem to serve no purpose. What are teens to do? This book is designed to help you answer some of those questions and understand your feelings. It will give you goals that will help you maintain order in your life and achieve the happiness intended for you.

Knowledge can help you understand your feelings and questions. Then, using this knowledge, you can cooperate with God and His grace so that you can learn to follow His plan for your happiness.

In this unit you will discover God's great plan for us, how the plan unraveled, and how a new understanding can help renew the world, one teen at a time. The teen years are ones of great idealism. Teens can see some of the problems of the world and set out to fix them with great energy. Spiritual and practical goals will be presented as a means of directing these energies toward good, which is how God desires them to be used. This will make a joyful and productive life a reachable goal instead of an impossible dream.

Chapter

One WHAT'S IT ALL ABOUT?
—God has given us the gifts of love and life through our family.
—The virtue of chastity helps protect love and life from selfishness and aggressiveness.
—For a fulfilling adult life, we must learn now to use these gifts of love and life in a way that is pleasing to God.

Chapter

TWO PUTTING THINGS IN ORDER
—God is the center and source of our existence.
—We must be great lovers like Jesus Christ.
—Sexual maturity is the ability to express ourselves as men or women in a way that will glorify God and serve His people.

Chapter

Three THE GREAT BREAK-UP
—Adam and Eve's disobedience broke our bond with God.
—As a result of the "big break-up", man's perfect order turned to chaos.
—The consequence of the fall, sin, can be seen in our culture.

WHAT'S IT ALL ABOUT?

- What is love?
- What is the purpose of life?

These questions are important to ask ourselves as we grow and develop from child to adult. During the teen years, our minds expand to seek and find a reason for all that we do. The answer to the question "Why did God make me?" is something you may have memorized as a child. If so, you know that the reason God gave us life is to know, love and serve Him in this world and be happy with Him eternally.

As we enter the teen years, we also need directions for adulthood. After all, we won't rely on parents forever! While we still live with them, we need to figure out the basics of adult living. *How* do I love? *How* do I live? Will I choose to live only for myself? Or will I choose to live for God? Can love be real if I live only for myself? Hey, that's a lot to think about!

God has freely given you love and life through your parents. Your family is the primary setting to learn about love and life. Ideally, your family is providing these daily lessons in a way that nurtures your growth to be a more loving person. Parents, brothers, sisters, relatives and family friends help us grow and provide us with opportunities to learn about love. When we experience their love, we taste God's commitment of love for us. The family is our first school of love.

Not everyone lives with two parents who are able to provide good care, however. Divorce, alcohol abuse and other tragedies harm family life.

Pope John Paul II spent many years teaching us about the family and how we can build a culture of love. He also reminded us that the devil, who cannot attack God Himself, is attacking family life, one of the most beautiful gifts God has given us. Besides the difficulties of families, an effort is underway to redefine the family—contradicting the One who invented families in the first place. It could get confusing! While none of our families is perfect, we still belong to families that God has given us, and we love them. And with the help of God's grace, we can all help build a civilization of love.

So far, because of our age and our needs, most of our family life experiences of love have been on the receiving end. Do you ever gratefully think about all you have freely received?

List some of the things you need in your life that God freely gives you:

_____

_____

_____

_____

_____

List things you need that your parents give you:

_____

_____

_____

_____

_____

When you were much younger, you accepted these gifts of love without returning them. Hopefully, in growing older you began to share your love with others. Now you share your affection, your joys, and your talents with family, friends and classmates. You are happy when you know that you've pleased others. Growing in unselfish love is necessary, so that as we mature, we choose to give our

lives in service to God and His people. As you prepare yourself to grow into adulthood, it is also important to learn more about God's plan for love and life. This course is designed to teach you how to follow the plan of God, so you can grow to maturity and live the fullness of life.

During adolescence you experience many changes that will help you share your love and life more deeply. Because you are a man or a woman, you are also a sexual being. Your sexuality is the way you express yourself as a man or as a woman—spiritually, physically, mentally, emotionally and socially. **In faithfulness to your baptismal promises, it is your responsibility to love as a man or a woman in the way that conforms to God's plan for you.** The virtue that helps you live out the responsibility to love is the virtue of chastity.

Chastity is the virtue that moderates our sexual desires in accordance with God's plan for us. In his teachings on family life, Pope John Paul II wrote: "Chastity is the spiritual energy capable of

> The virtue of chastity gives us the freedom to love the way God wants us to.

defending love from the perils of selfishness and aggressiveness; and advancing love toward its full realization." Chastity is sexual self-control. Chastity —a spiritual energy—helps us love as God commands us to love. The virtue of chastity helps us protect our love from misuse. Chastity is the way to true love.

The opposite of chastity is uncontrolled sexual behavior, or lust, one of the seven capital sins. To use our sexual powers for selfish pleasure or to join ourselves to another outside of the union of marriage are sins against chastity.

The family was given to us by God when He created Adam and Eve. "Male and female he created them. And God blessed them, and God said to them,

'Be fruitful and multiply, and fill the earth and subdue it . . .' " (Genesis 1:27–28). The Scriptures tell us that God established the family as a man and a woman, joined in marriage to become one flesh and have children. As human beings created by God, we have no power to change His definition of the family. The family is an institution designed by God. It is a community of love by which God continues His creation of human life. God's laws for marriage were given to Moses in about 1200 B.C. They are found in the sixth and ninth commandments:

SIXTH   You shall not commit adultery.
NINTH   You shall not covet your
              neighbor's wife.

We are commanded to purity of the body in the sixth commandment and purity of mind in the ninth commandment. "You shall not commit adultery" means that it is wrong for us to use our sexual powers outside of marriage. Doing that violates the sacredness and dignity of sex, and the dignity of the human person. The ninth commandment, "You shall not covet your neighbor's wife", means that we do not dwell upon sexual thoughts or desires when they enter into our minds. Instead, we use our imaginations to start thinking of something else that is true or good or beautiful or funny—or at least distracting.

When Jesus brought us the New Law, to love others as He has loved us, He challenged us to an even greater purity. "But I say to you that everyone who looks at a woman lustfully has already committed adultery with her in his heart" (Matthew 5:28).

No doubt, Jesus is calling us to be pure and chaste. "Blessed are the pure of heart; for they shall see God" (Matthew 5:8). He knows purity is a challenge for us. But we are **not alone!** God is with us. He offers us help through the Church, which He established. Christ has shown us in the Gospels how we should live, and the Holy Spirit continues to strengthen us to love God and our neighbor.

Since God invented male and female, it makes sense that we go to Him to learn the truth about sexual love. God has a plan for the proper use of sexuality in love giving and life giving. To ignore or disobey His plan is a serious abuse of ourselves and others, and it is a sin. Sin harms us and others. Sin is the opposite of love because God is Love.

The difference between use and abuse also applies to many other gifts from God. For example, the proper use of food would be

- Eating a balanced and nutritious diet
- Eating the right amounts by practicing self-control
- Storing and disposing of food in a proper way

These uses of food nourish us. The abuse of food may include

- Overeating
- Eating too much junk food
- Eating compulsively to escape problems
- Bulimia or anorexia

List proper uses and abuses for the following:

	PROPER USE (helps life)	ABUSE (harms life)
Electricity:		
Water:		
Fire:		
Sexual activity:		

We do need food, but we do not need to overeat or eat junk food. So we need to develop the virtue of temperance, or moderation. With sexuality it is a little different. We cannot live without food, but we *can* live without sexual activity. We do need to live as the masculine or feminine person God created us to be, but we do not need sexual activity at all outside of marriage. In fact, sexual activity is harmful to unmarried people. And even married people need to express their love for each other according to God's plan.

Yet, God's call to chastity is even bigger than restraining our behavior. It is about our integrity, our wholeness, and the meaning of our life. The *Catechism of the Catholic Church,* no. 2338, states: "The chaste person maintains the integrity of the powers of life and love placed in him. This integrity ensures the unity of the person; it is opposed to any behavior that would impair it."

So, the reason for this book is to help you understand, in the light of Christ, the need for chastity. Many social and moral issues will be presented here in the *Student Guide*. Some of the more delicate or private matters are in the *Parent Guide* that accompanies this book. Some details and extra questions are answered for your parents in their guidebook, so you can learn the more intimate lessons of love and life from them. Overall, the course can help you learn to live the wholeness, or integrity, of the human person that God made us to be, through developing and practicing the virtue of chastity.

Let's journey together through these instructions on Christian sexual morality, so we can diminish our fears and curiosities and focus on living and loving as a reflection of God's love.

I'm still not sure what this is all about.

I guess we'd better find out more about chastity then.

Well, Chastity is God's plan for Love and Life.

Maybe "putting things in order" will help.

PUTTING THINGS IN ORDER

As we have seen, chastity is part of our wholeness and our holiness. Chaste sexuality is the successful integration of body and spirit. God has given us guidance in living as a fully integrated male or female person. Sexual maturity results from knowing and living the truth that certain human sexual expressions are reserved only for marriage.

We live in a culture that is full of messages that promote the wrong ideas about sexuality. Movies, magazine articles and product ads lead us to believe that sexuality is only about the body. But as children of God, we are made of body and soul. So the last thing we should do to learn the truth about love and life is rely on movies, magazines and popular music. There are very few examples of true love in the secular media.

The culture that we live in presents a *disordered* view of sexuality and sexual expression. This disorder has caused a lot of unhappiness. It is easy to get confused without clear directions. To help us understand, let's take an example from astronomy.

Back in the second century, an astronomer named Ptolemy presented a theory of our planetary system that showed the sun and moon revolving around the earth. From our position on earth, the theory was believable. For many centuries, astronomers tried to prove that this theory was true. However, they realized there were too many inconsistencies and unanswered questions. So they continued to search for a different theory of the universe, although most people believed Ptolemy's theory for a very long time.

Now we know differently, but suppose your teacher brought a five-year-old girl into your classroom and offered to give you $500 if you could convince her that the earth is the center of the uni-

Immature Theory: The earth is the center of the universe.

verse. Would you take that offer, even knowing it was a lie? Why would you do it?

- For the money?
- Because five-year-olds are naive, and they'll believe anything?
- For the money?
- Because she is not old enough to know any better?
- For the money?
- Because it seems true, and five-year-olds don't know the whole story of the solar system; they only know what they can see now?

Wouldn't you call this exploitation?

Since you are older, you wouldn't fall for Ptolemy's theory. You know the truth. So let's treat the five-year-old right and label the parts of the solar system correctly.

Copernicus discovered the true order of the solar system in the sixteenth century. As we began

to see his theory in motion, everything else seemed to take on more meaning. In God's magnificent design there's good reason for the sun being in the center. The sun is the source of energy, light and heat. It holds the earth in orbit with its gravity, so we can't go spinning off into space. Now this system makes sense!

What's Happening Today?

If you are younger than thirty, as long as you have been alive you have seen or heard movies, TV shows, books, songs and magazines that proclaim sex is the center of the universe.

Well, that's what the media are teaching, isn't it? Is that an immature notion or a mature notion? Is that the truth, or a falsehood?

Yet, if someone were to offer you millions of dollars to convince young people that this was true, why would you take up the offer?

Immature Theory:

All the pleasure you seek, and more!

Excitement! Passion! More skin than you can believe!

What happens in Las Vegas, stays in Las Vegas.

- For the money?
  (Teens have money and no bills to pay yet.)
- Because teens are just beginning to experience their sexuality and they'll listen to the loudest voice?
- For the money?
- Because young people are inexperienced in life, and they can see things from only one perspective?
- For the money?
- Because teens' bodies can be lured and their minds have not matured?

Are you going to fall for the media's message? Do you call this exploitation?

What Is the Mature Notion of Human Sexuality?

God, Who is Love, is the center, source and purpose of our existence. Our natures gravitate toward God. Unless God is the center of our lives, there are many inconsistencies and unanswered questions, as well as much unhappiness. There is

an emptiness that can be filled only by God, Who is our source of energy and light, life and love.

The mature notion of human sexuality helps us to understand many ways by which we can receive and give God's love and thereby demonstrate His love to the world. Whether our vocation is to marriage, priesthood or consecrated life, we can be great lovers in the same way that God is a great lover.

Label the diagram below with God as the center and with the planets as marriage, priesthood and consecrated religious life. God thinks it is so important for us to learn to be great lovers that He sent His Son, Jesus, to show us the way of love. Love is forgiveness. Love is self-sacrifice. Love is obedience. Love is other-centered.

Putting things in order allows us to see where sexuality belongs. God has placed sexual activity

within marriage to express a total commitment of love giving and life giving. Sexual activity is only one of the many aspects of marriage. Others are generosity, understanding, forgiveness, sacrifice and even picking up someone else's dirty socks, *cheerfully*. Sexual activity is not the only expression of love in marriage, but marriage is the only place where it belongs.

As we begin to see the way God has ordered His creation, we begin to understand and respect His plan for sexuality. Our acceptance of God's order is the beginning of sexual maturity.

God's love (not sex) is the center of life!

Sexual maturity is being able to express yourself as a man or woman according to God's plan.

- Knowing what is pure and good
- Living chastely according to your vocation

That definition sounds a lot like chastity, doesn't it?

Yeah, I guess chastity and maturity go together.

PROJECTS

1. Bring in an advertisement from a magazine or newspaper that uses sex appeal to sell the product. Recreate an ad for that product which does not exploit God's plan for sexuality.

2. Make your ad into a short TV commercial or song and videotape it; or use pictures of yourself, friends or family members, or original artwork to create the ad in a magazine style.

3. Write your own advertisement. Many of you have creative minds that are just waiting to be discovered. Here's your chance to do something good. Write an advertisement for doing something good:

   - Being honest
   - Helping someone
   - Stopping a fight
   - Being kind
   - Living God's plan for sexuality
   - Practicing patience

4. *Yes* or *No*

   - Is it important to have sex appeal? _____
   - Is it important to dress modestly? _____
   - Did God create male and female? _____
   - Were we created to reflect God's love? _____
   - Does sexuality belong in marriage? _____
   - As long as the two people agree, is anything OK? _____
   - Should we follow God's way to be happy? _____
   - Does happiness come from doing only what you want to do? _____
   - Does God love you more than any human person ever can? _____
   - Do television advertisers care about you? _____

THE GREAT BREAK-UP

God gave us our sexuality so that we could both give and receive His life-giving love and participate in His creation. But you'd never know this from watching TV or movies. What happened that turned this good gift of God into something so disordered?

The Fall

When God created Adam and Eve, He gave them a free will. That means that they had the freedom to *choose* to obey, love and serve Him. God made humans different from the animals. Animals were designed to serve God automatically by instinct. Of course, for our choice to be real, there has to be more than one thing to choose from. Adam and Eve could choose either to obey God or to disobey Him. We all know which choice they made, but let's take a closer look at how it happened.

The serpent tried to make God's command look ridiculous to Eve, first by misquoting God and then by putting doubt in Eve's mind. So, Eve and Adam fell for his tricks. This was the original sin.

Now the serpent was the most cunning of all the animals that the Lord God had made.

"Did God really tell you not to eat from any of the trees in the garden?"

"We may eat of the fruit of the trees in the garden; it is only about the fruit of the tree in the middle of the garden that God said, 'You shall not eat it or even touch it, lest you die.'"

"You certainly will not die! No, God knows well that the moment you eat of it you will be like gods who know what is good and what is bad."

The Result

When sin entered the world our bond with God was broken, the order of God's creation was disrupted and our inner peace and joy were destroyed. Everything became more difficult. It became easier to sin than to be good. Our wills were weakened and our minds were darkened. Sometimes we get confused between right and wrong when parents or teachers, or other guides are not there to remind us. Even though we have a conscience that tells us to follow God, it would be more difficult to choose right over wrong if God did not remind us and support us through His Church.

Human beings, who were in perfect communion with God before the Fall, now struggle to pay attention in prayer. They may be tempted to doubt God's wisdom or even His existence. Man and woman, who were made for each other, now are tempted to criticize and compete rather than harmonize their different talents. A man and woman who would have looked at one another with tenderness and gratitude before the Fall may now be tempted to manipulate or to use one another for selfish reasons.

Since Adam and Eve disobeyed God, all of their children, including ourselves, are tempted to disobey God, too. Now do you see why your parents wanted to baptize you as an infant? They wanted that original sin washed from your soul so that you could live in God's grace. Yet, due to our weakness, we sometimes choose to sin. Even little sins can destroy our inner peace. We can find peace only in union with God, and we have to seek that union. Those moments are not always easy to find, but we must try.

Regardless of the kind of sin we commit, the result is that we spoil God's gifts. We no longer enjoy a natural control over things like hate, anger and laziness. We no longer enjoy the inner harmony God wants us to have. We feel emptiness inside, and

we may try to fill it with all the wrong things. We even do this with our physical emptiness of hunger. For example, we may eat lots of junk food instead of eating the good things our body needs. Some people may try to fill their need for love and affection with sexual activity instead of friendship. Some people may even set up sexual attraction as a false god, thinking it will make them happy, give their lives meaning or solve their problems. People who give in to sexual temptations begin to confuse love with lust. All these effects of sin lead to confusion, living according to feelings instead of living according to our identity as children of God. Happy families become unhappy. Unhappy families give up and break up. Many sad consequences are the result of original sin and our actual sins.

The Pressures Around Us

We have seen that one of the effects of original sin is that we lost control over our desires. Instead of desiring only what is good for us, we suffer from disordered desires for what is harmful to us. Now we have to fight with our mind and will to regain control over our desires and seek God's grace to lead us in the right direction. But that fight is made even more difficult by the pressures around us. One of these pressures is the media. Think of all the commercials that encourage us to "Buy now!" "Don't put it off!" or ask, "Why deny yourself?" Or consider the messages the media give us about sex: "Adultery is beautiful." "Everyone is doing it." Pornography is waiting to jump into our computer to tempt us, too—its whole purpose is to get our sexual drives out of control and train us to use people for pleasure instead of loving them.

Today's Popular Music: The Message

Today's secular world tries to twist God's good gifts and to cause us to lose control. Sometimes we encounter this through TV shows and movies that make sin look attractive. At other times it comes through the music that we allow to play over and over in our heads. It's important to be able to see through the deception, so we can avoid being brainwashed with the world's lies about sexuality and relationships.

Select a popular song to analyze; see what effect you think such music may have on you.

(1) The Analysis

A. **OVERALL MESSAGE**
- Is the message of the song basically moral, immoral or amoral (has no morality)?
- Is it in conflict with the Christian message, or is it expressing the same message as Christ?
- Does it encourage acceptance of sexually immoral thoughts or behavior?
- Does it strengthen or cheapen the dignity of persons?
- If you have seen the music-video for this song, what does it show?

Wait a second! I thought he said this was a song about love? That guy on the stage just bit the head off a bird and hit a girl in the face with his electric guitar! Now what's love got to do with *that*?!

- Do you think the performing artist is a positive inspiration to young people? Why or why not?

(2) **The Challenge**

   A. If you were a parent, would you like your teenager to be influenced by this song?

   B. After you've finished writing your answers to the previous questions, ask your parents what they think of this song.

   C. What words or phrases would you change to make the message more helpful to Christian teens?

(3) **Your Opinion**

   A. Teenage music has been criticized by older people since before the invention of rock 'n' roll. Do you think this criticism is justified? Why or why not?

   B. In recent years, more criticism has come not just from parents, but from psychologists and sociologists. They claim that much of today's music promotes violence and immoral sex. They say this new music is more damaging than the music of the past. Do you agree or disagree? Give examples and reasons for your answer.

   C. Many young people who listen to or watch songs suggestive of immorality say that they just like the beat, and that they don't pay attention to the words. Do you think this is true? Do you think they would like the songs just as much if there were no words in them, or if the same message was used by a Christian rock group with a more positive message? And what about the beat, does it help or hinder self-control?

B. FEELINGS

- Does the song help you to understand your own feelings?
- Do the words suggest that actions be based only on feelings?
- Does the beat of the music stir feelings or desires?

C. LOVE

- What does the song say about love?
- Does it confuse "love" with infatuation, romance, or sexual passion? (Remember that real love is "other-centered". It means caring for the happiness and life of the other person, even if this happiness does not include you. Love is patient, kind, forgiving and self-sacrificing.)
- Does the message encourage selfishness, which is the opposite of love?
- What would Jesus, the greatest lover, say about this song?

D. THE EFFECT

- Do you think the (direct or indirect) messages in the song are a help to Christian teens? Why or why not?

Now What?

So where does all this leave us? What can be done about the mess that sin has made of our world and our lives? God did punish Adam and Eve for their sin; a just God couldn't simply ignore what they had done.

But He didn't abandon them; He is also merciful and loving. Because God loves us so much, He didn't want us to be bound by sin. God gave us hope by promising us a Savior to bridge the gap between God and man. The next chapter will show us how God fulfilled His promise to free us from the slavery of sin.

Consider each of the conditions described in this list. Put a check by those that describe what life was like before the Fall of Adam and Eve. Refer to the book of Genesis if you need help.

____ Eating only enough to satisfy your needs
____ Living in perfect harmony with nature
____ Work is difficult
____ Tendency to laziness
____ Constant communication with God
____ Animals will harm you
____ Passions are easily controlled by the mind
____ Our greatest pleasure is being in the presence of God
____ We are self-conscious

> God has given us free will so that we can *choose* to obey, love and serve Him.

Before the Fall	After the Fall (The state of original sin)
The intellect and will together guided the passions and body. We "had it together" with all the virtues and graces. We had perfect self-mastery.	The intellect was darkened and the will was weakened. Now we suffer from disordered desires instead of desiring only what is good for us.

THE GREAT MAKE-UP

For I delight in the law of God, in my inmost self, but I see in my members another law at war with the law of my mind and making me captive to the law of sin which dwells in my members. Wretched man that I am! Who will deliver me from this body of death? Thanks be to God through Jesus Christ our Lord! (Romans 7:22–25a)

After the Fall we were left with a situation that looked something like this:

The separation between God and us could not be mended by anything we could do ourselves. But the same God we rejected loved us so much that He provided a solution. He sent Jesus to make God real to us; Jesus is God "in the flesh", the Incarnation.

God taught us everything we need to know about Himself in the simplest way possible—human words and actions. Christ is the clearest expression of God's message. He not only became man because He loves us, He also died on the Cross because He loves us.

> God's Love Is More
> Powerful Than Sin

The Main Event

Jesus is the "bridge" promised to Adam and Eve. He came to give us a way back to God. How did He do this? By His passion, death and Resurrection. Christ proved His love for us in the most perfect way possible. Now it's up to us to walk across this bridge by accepting and imitating Jesus Christ, who is Love.

Christ as Our Example

Christ lived through many situations that we also experience, giving us the example of how to deal with them. Read these incidents in Jesus' life and describe a similar situation in your life.

1. Jesus obediently returns home with His parents when they find Him teaching in the temple (Luke 2:46–52).

_____

_____

2. Jesus weeps when He hears that His friend Lazarus has died (John 11:33–38).

_____

_____

3. Jesus is tempted by Satan (Matthew 4:1–11).

_____

_____

4. Jesus is justifiably angry with the money changers in the temple (John 2:13–17).

_____

_____

5. Jesus calms the storm (Matthew 8:23–27).

_____

_____

6. Jesus washes the feet of His Apostles at the Last Supper (John 13:1–17).

_____

_____

Another important lesson we can learn from Jesus is forgiveness. Christ forgave those who crucified Him even while He was hanging from the Cross. We should work at forgiving and then forgetting the slights and injustices we suffer. We need to remember that we, too, are in need of forgiveness.

By forgiving others we show them the love we ourselves need and receive freely from God.

Next time you are tempted to hate someone, remember Christ thought that person worth dying for.

The Joy of Redemption

Surrounded by messages that tell us to seek only pleasure and comfort, we Christians must strive to learn the meaning of pain and death. Without Good Friday there is no Easter Sunday. The meaning of Jesus' suffering and death becomes clear when we believe in the Resurrection. Christ's Resurrection three days after His death is the cornerstone of our faith and is proof, through the eyes of faith, that Jesus is God. God Our Father can bring good even out of suffering and death. Because of Christ, the suffering in our lives also can be lifted up to God and transformed into a source of grace for ourselves and others.

> Maturity = Ability to Forgive

Sharing in Christ's Suffering

Read Matthew, chapters 26 and 27, and then identify the sufferings of Jesus that can provide us with an example for the following situations. The first one is done for you.

1. People at school are jealous of Sara's intelligence and make fun of her.
   The soldiers mock Jesus.
   _____

2. Mike feels that some of his parents' requests are unreasonable.
   _____
   _____

3. Anne's friend spreads an unflattering story about her.
   _____
   _____

4. One of Craig's teachers has penalized him for something he did not even do.
   _____
   _____

5. Beth's parents have given her a curfew that requires her to be home while most of her friends are still out.
   _____
   _____

Redeemed Person, Redeemed Sexuality

Because Jesus Christ redeemed us, we have the power to reject the unloving ways of the world and to follow the path of God. Adam and Eve fell for Satan's lies, but because of the restoration of grace, we don't have to fall for the lies of Satan or of our culture. Jesus redeemed all of us from the disorder that was caused by sin, so we do not have to be slaves to sin. We have the grace—through the redemption—to overcome the temptation to sin. He gives us the grace to live in harmony with Him, if only we turn to Him. He redeemed the whole person, including our sexuality, so that we can properly express His love to the world. Jesus Christ can fill our hearts with His love now, so that we don't have to run around searching for another person, thing, activity or idea to fill our emptiness.

Christians can live fully and freely because of the death and Resurrection of Jesus Christ. We do this by following in the footsteps of Christ and trying to imitate Him with our lives. This will make us happy because we were made in the image and likeness of God.

THE REAL SOURCE AND THE REAL FORCE

Man fell and was lost. Jesus Christ not only redeemed us, but founded a Church to be our Christian family here on earth. The Church will help keep us from getting lost, support us in our efforts to be good, and provide for our spiritual needs through the sacraments.

Is the only purpose for a family to make rules for us to follow? Well, it may seem that way when you are a teen hoping for more freedom, but it's really not true. God gave us families to love us. God's plan is that we should be conceived in love and raised in love. Even if other circumstances disrupt family life, the guidance, support and love of our parents have helped make each of us the kind of person he is today. Our parents have shown their love for us in countless ways. Daily they work hard to provide for our needs. They care for us when we are sick and help us with our struggles. If they love us this much, the chances are good that their rules

exist to help us become the best that we can be and not to make us miserable.

In the spiritual sphere Christ also gave us parents and a family. He knew that we couldn't make it on our own, so He joined us together with Him through the Holy Spirit to give us guidance and love in the Church. In the Church, all of us are united to each other and to Christ through our Baptism. Through the Church and the Eucharist, Christ comes to us and lives in us. When we allow Him to live in us, He also comes into the world again *through* us and through our actions of service to others.

St. Paul calls the Church the Mystical Body of Christ. Christ is the head, and we each have our particular jobs as parts of His Body. Even if you are only the little finger, the hand cannot function properly without you. Your job in the Church is unique and necessary.

Each of us has a particular role to play in the Mystical Body. Just as when something good happens to you and you feel good all over, so when you do something good for the sake of another person, the whole Body of Christ benefits.

Think of the last good thing you did for someone. Did it make that person happy? Did it make others happy as well? What would have happened to that person, or to the others, if you had not done something good for that person at the moment?

Belonging to Christ's Mystical Body is important for all involved.

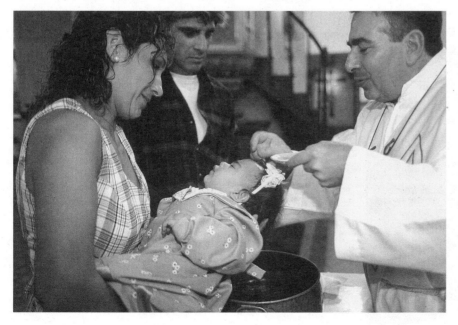

Explain how you benefit by being
a member of Christ's Mystical Body.

_____

_____

_____

Explain how the Body of Christ can
benefit by your membership and participation.

_____

_____

_____

The Sacraments

In your family, your parents' love for you is shown
in all that they do to take care of you. They feed,
clothe and shelter you. They instruct, encourage and
guide you. Through His Church, Christ also shows
us His love. Through the teachings of the Church,
He gives us wisdom, and through the seven sacraments He gives nourishment to our souls.

**The sacraments are outward signs instituted
by Christ to give grace.** Grace is God's own supernatural life, which He shares with us so that we might
become like Him. All life, all love comes from God.
He is the one and only force for good. He is the one

and only source of good. And He makes Himself
available to us through the sacraments.

Just as we have physical, intellectual and emotional needs that must be met in order for us to live a
fully human life, so also we have spiritual needs that
must be met. Remember, a human person is both a
body and a soul. And along with our bodies, our
souls go through various stages of development—
birth, childhood, and maturity—as we grow more
and more into the likeness of God.

This is not to say that our bodies and souls
grow at exactly the same rate. A man can be bap-
tized on his deathbed. Though old in body, his soul
can be born anew. In the Eastern churches, Baptism,
Confirmation and Eucharist are given to infants.
With this qualification in mind, the sacraments can
be seen as corresponding to human growth.

See if you can match the sacraments with periods or
needs of human development. Confirmation is done
for you.

SOCIAL DEVELOPMENT AND PHYSICAL NEEDS	SACRAMENTS
Being born	Confirmation
Sustaining with food	Baptism
Giving witness to the truth	Penance
Seeking forgiveness	Matrimony
Nearing death	Eucharist
Being spouses and parents	Anointing the sick

Our relationship with God begins in Baptism
when God comes to live in our souls. Our bodies are
homes for God and temples of the same Holy Spirit
Who is in Christ. We have dignity because we are
made in the image of God. This dignity is magnified
when we invite God to live within us by properly
receiving the sacraments.

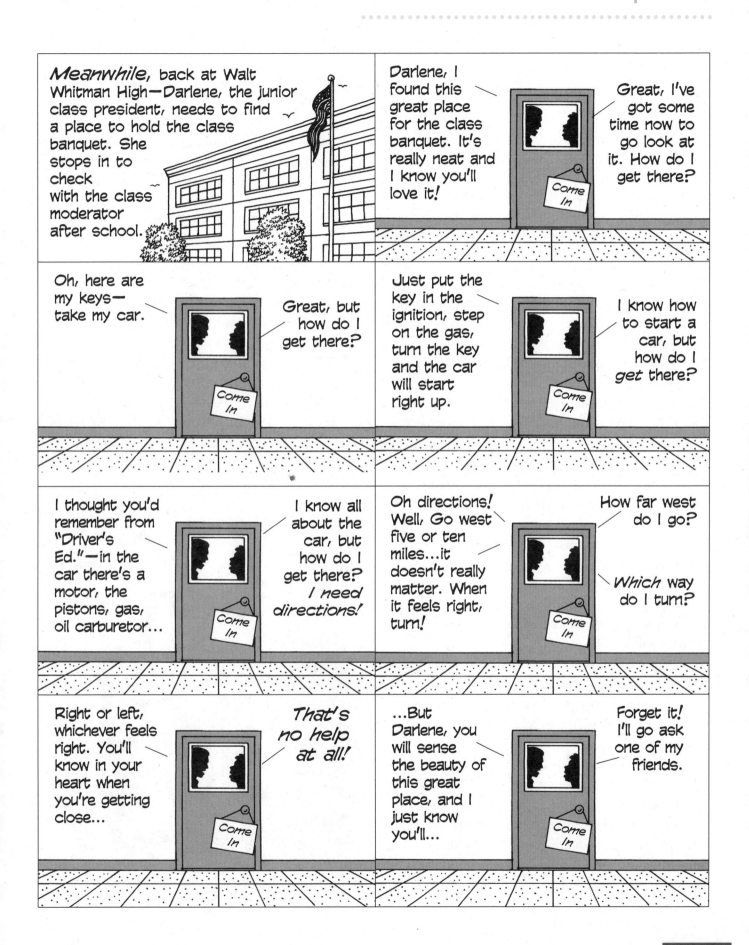

Household Rules

In most homes there are certain "rules and regulations" that your parents enforce because they love you. Even though these rules are not always welcomed with open arms, they are necessary because they help the household run smoothly and they help us to grow and mature. Your parents likely have wisdom and experience that you don't yet fully appreciate.

Free Directions

What if we had no Church and no guidance from home? What if we had to figure everything out for ourselves and then suffer the consequences of our own mistakes? We'd probably say, "C'mon, God. That's not fair. We need more help than that! This is a crazy world!"

What a great God we have! Christ founded the Church to help us—to give us guidance and to protect us from too much confusion and failure.

The Church's rules are the teachings of Christ. These teachings help us live as Christians. Because of His great love for us, Christ sent the Holy Spirit to guide the popes and bishops through the ages. As members of the Church we benefit from the guidance of the Holy Spirit as well as the wisdom and experience of all times. Through the knowledge of Sacred Tradition and the Holy Scriptures, we can inform our consciences with **truth**.

People opposed to Christ may tempt us with a contrary view. They may say that no matter what we do God will take us to Heaven, which is the sin of presumption. Presumption is a great lie that Satan might whisper in your ears as you grow into independence and adulthood. After all, Satan's whole plan is to get you away from God. The lies of Satan might sound pleasing to our fallen nature because it certainly seems easier to make up our own way rather than follow God's plan for us. Remember that this is what misled Adam and Eve. Their sin didn't lead them to freedom or happiness, but quite the opposite.

Christ showed us that the best way is not the easiest. Don't fall for lies! We can't "take it easy" in our faith!

The choice for Christ will always be a challenge, but we have the Holy Spirit, given to the Church at Pentecost and to us through the Sacraments, to guide us. We will be tempted with reasons for not being good or with excuses for not confessing our sins, but God, who is Perfect Love, Perfect Mercy and Perfect Justice, will always give us what we truly need if we but only ask.

Our belonging to Christ began at our Baptism. When we received Baptism, we were incorporated into the Mystical Body of Christ and were given the Holy Spirit. We became adopted children of God. All we need to do is take good care of the graces that are constantly sent our way to nourish and strengthen us. That is what will make it easier to follow the real rules. You belong to Christ. You will be much happier if you remain close to Him.

FOOTPRINTS IN THE SAND

One night a man had a dream. He dreamed
he was walking along the beach with the Lord.
Across the sky flashed scenes from his life.
For each scene he noticed two sets of
footprints in the sand; one belonging
to him, and the other to the Lord.
When the last scene of his life flashed
before him, he looked back at the
footprints in the sand.
He noticed that many times along the path of
his life there was only one set of footprints.
He also noticed that it happened at the very
lowest and saddest times in his life.
This really bothered him and he
questioned the Lord about it.
"Lord, you said that once I decided to follow
you, you'd walk with me all the way.
But I have noticed that during the most
troublesome times in my life,
there is only one set of footprints.
I don't understand why when
I needed you most you would leave me."
The Lord replied,
"My precious, precious child,
I love you and I would never leave you.
During your times of trial and suffering,
when you see only one set of footprints,
it was then that I carried you."

— Mary Stevenson

God help me
And lead me
Down the road to You.

Give me strength
To go on
And live my life with You.

You give me
Laws, signs, love;
Help me show
The love I have for You.

—Jackie, 17

Thank God for the Church!

The Church is the real source of the real force. The
Love and Life of God initiated all of existence. God
gives us His love and life through the Church.

So if you're looking for love, where should you
look? In the computer? On the TV? In a romance
novel? Or in the Church?

Christ showed us the way of real love. He lived
and died and rose for us and established His Church
to guide us. He gave St. Peter the keys to the

Kingdom of Heaven. Christ gave Peter the authority
to bind on earth what is bound in Heaven (see
Matthew 16:18–19). God passes on the authority to
teach faith and morals to each consecutive Pope.
The real rules of love can be found in the teachings
of the Catholic Church. No matter what is going on
in the culture, the society and the world, our Church
is here, guided by the light of the Holy Spirit, to
show us the way of love.

Even if many people reject the teachings of the
Church, those teachings are still the wisdom of God
that will bring you fulfillment. If what you are thinking of doing "seems right" or "you can't understand
why it's wrong", check with the *Catechism of the
Catholic Church* or go to the Vatican website
(http://www.vatican.va/). If you obey God first,
then you may understand later. If you don't obey,
you may never understand because sin can cloud
your judgment. The Church is here to help us learn
and understand, so we can experience God's love
while we are on earth and stay on the path to eternal
love and happiness.

GETTING IT TOGETHER

What do you remember?

PART I. MATCHING—Put the letter of the correct definition in the blank before the correct word.

1. _____ Chastity
2. _____ Grace
3. _____ Commitment
4. _____ Original sin
5. _____ Incarnation

6. _____ Exploitation
7. _____ Mystical Body of Christ
8. _____ Seven sacraments
9. _____ Baptism
10. _____ Family

A. A promise made between two people
B. The outward signs Christ left us as a means of giving us grace
C. The virtue that protects love from selfishness and aggressiveness
D. The sacrament by which we enter the family of Christ and begin our love relationship with Christ
E. God's supernatural life within us
F. The term used by St. Paul to describe all those people within the family of Christ and His Church
G. To use someone for our own gain or pleasure
H. The term for God's becoming man in Jesus Christ
I. Instituted by God as a married man and woman and their children
J. The sin committed by Adam and Eve, which we inherit because they were our first parents

PART II. FILL IN THE BLANK OR BLANKS—with the correct word or phrase to complete the meaning of these sentences. Each word will be used only once.

broke	free will
forgiveness	God
dignity	maturity
family	obedience
passion, death and Resurrection	protect

1. _____ gave us His love and life, to place at the center and source of our existence.

2. We learn our first lesson about God's love from our _____.

3. Sexual _____ is being able to express yourself as a man or woman in a way that glorifies God, serves His people and leads to true happiness.

4. When God created Adam and Eve, He gave them _____ so they could choose to love Him.

5. In disobeying God, Adam and Eve _____ their intimate bond with Him.

6. Christ's love in becoming man raised our human _____ even higher than it had been at Creation.

7. Christ taught us the importance of loving _____ to parents.

8. Christ bridged the gap between God and man by His _____ _____, His act of total love.

9. We must learn self-sacrifice and _____ from Christ's sufferings on the Cross.

10. The laws of Christ and His Church are given out of God's love for us.

   These laws are meant to help us be good and _____ us from harm.

PARENT–TEEN DISCUSSION
Questionnaire

This *Love and Life* program is designed to improve your relationship with your parents. Building relationships requires communication. The *Parent Guide* that accompanies this text gives background information and practical tips to help you and your parents talk to each other and discuss the topics presented in the program.

   Here is a questionnaire to help you begin. Think about the questions first and then discuss them with your parents.

1. How much time do you normally spend with your parents in a week?
   0–2 hrs.   2–4 hrs.   4–6 hrs.   6–8 hrs.   8 hrs. or more

2. How often do you talk to your parents about things that are bothering you? (Circle one.)   Never   Seldom   Often   Always

3. Can you talk openly and freely with your parents?

4. Do you talk about God and our Faith with your parents?

5. What have your parents done for you that you appreciate?

6. What do you do for your parents that you hope they appreciate?

7. Do you think you are given enough responsibility? If your answer is no, in what areas would you like more?

8. Have your parents talked with you about your concerns of growing up? If not, what topics would you like to discuss?

9. How can you and your parents improve your relationship?

THE BUILDING BLOCKS OF LOVE AND LIFE

How do we get from here—young teens trying to figure out the meaning of love and life—to where we want to be—in the vocation that will lead us to a fulfilling life on earth and eternal life with God? Whether your path will be marriage or celibacy, you will need to learn the building blocks of love and life. Without good building blocks, our lives can crumble.

Developing the virtue of chastity is a lot more than avoiding passionate kissing and keeping all our clothes fastened. Chastity is part of an overall life of virtue; learning and practicing Christian love, developing true friendships, growing in emotional maturity and practicing self-control are foundations for chastity. On the other hand, without chastity, it is almost impossible to learn these essential building blocks for relationships of love and life.

Chapter
Six MALE AND FEMALE HE CREATED THEM
—God created us in His own image, male and female.
—Growing to appreciate the opposite sex helps prepare us for adulthood.
—God gave a holy assignment to married men and women: to become one in love while being open to life.

Chapter
Seven A LIFE OF VIRTUE
—A virtuous life is our response to God's love.
—God wants you to develop your gifts and talents as only you can.
—You can grow in character by changing your bad habits one at a time.

Chapter
Eight A LIFE OF LOVE
—God commands, not suggests, that we love Him and love our neighbor.
—We must practice Christ-like love every day.
—Rating our ability to love can help us see ways to grow.

Chapter

Nine A LIFE OF FRIENDSHIP

—God wants us to have good friends and be good friends.

—Friends should influence each other for good, which is God's plan.

—Planning activities can help us have constructive fun.

Chapter

Ten A LIFE OF EMOTIONAL MATURITY

—The emotionally mature stop to think before they act.

—Feelings can help us make decisions, but our decisions should not be based on them.

—Those who have practiced emotional maturity all along have an easier time managing the new sexual feelings during the teen years.

Chapter

Eleven PUT YOURSELF IN THE DRIVER'S SEAT — WITH SELF-MASTERY!

—God created us with certain drives and desires for a specific purpose.

—Along with our physical desires comes the responsibility of guiding our instincts with our intellect and will.

—God's grace is an extra force to help our self-control.

MALE AND FEMALE HE CREATED THEM

The words *sex* and *sexuality* can get people's attention. When you think of the word *sex*, do you associate God with it? Some people who have been exposed to the world's idea of sexuality might automatically associate sex with X-ratings, dirty jokes or perversion.

Is it possible to see our sexuality as something beautiful? God does. Did you ever think of looking to God for answers to your questions about sexuality? After all, sex was His idea in the first place. As Christians, we can see and live God's good plan for chastity and sexuality, as well as share that good news with others.

When we speak of sexuality, we are talking about our maleness or femaleness, something much greater than a physical act.

Sexuality is a fundamental part of our being. Our masculinity or femininity is expressed physically, psychologically, socially and emotionally. The *Catechism* states that "Everyone, man and woman, should acknowledge and accept his sexual *identity*" (*CCC* 2333). Sexuality is a basic part of our personality, the way we communicate with others, the way we feel, the way we express our human love and the way we progress toward maturity as a male or female person. God created us male and female. He said it is good.

Created in the Image of God

In His great love for us, God created us in His Image. Although we have bodies, He did not make us like the lower animals or plants. Although we have rational souls, we are not just like the angels. We are a composite being: We have a physical body and we have a spiritual dimension, a gift of God that He shared only with human beings and angels. Because of our souls, we can think, choose and express the unique male or female personhood God assigned to us. We can mirror God's love through our bodily actions. Our bodies are the vehicles through which we speak the spiritual and physical language of love through our thoughts, words and deeds.

Our sexuality especially affects our capacity to love others and to give life through procreation. Procreation is joining our lives with God's life to help in the act of creation. Procreation is co-creating new life with God. In God's plan, new human life

> So God created man in his own image, in the image of God he created him; male and female he created them. And God blessed them, and God said to them, "Be fruitful and multiply, and fill the earth and subdue it; and have dominion over the fish of the sea and over the birds of the air and over every living thing that moves upon the earth."
>
> —Genesis 1:27–28

comes into the world through a bond of love of a husband and wife.

The Bible tells us that God created us male and female because He saw that it was not good for man to be alone. He created us male and female to complete and complement each other. You may be familiar with complementary colors or complementary foods. They are different but go well together, just as do the complementary sexes, male and female. Man and woman together are created in the image of God and can express His goodness and wisdom. God made woman from the side of man, showing the equal dignity of men and women.

The Book of Genesis also tells us that God made man and woman to be the perfect partners for each other. Man delighted in the goodness of his partner when he first met Eve, before original sin, of course. Each was a unique person, but their differences complemented one another. They shared God's love through all facets of their being, including their sexuality.

Male and Female, He Created Them

God assigned our sex at the moment of conception. The set of chromosomes we received determined whether we are male or female. These sexual differ-ences are present in every cell of our body and influence our body structure, growth and chemistry.

Questions about your sex were probably the first ones asked after your birth: "Boy or girl?" The doctor and your family answered with excitement. You remained that boy or girl through childhood and displayed your "boyishness or girlishness" in your thoughts and actions. It doesn't take long for children to notice that boys are physically different from girls, too. Later on, they also notice that there are many other differences. All of this is part of God's plan for us—to be different, but equal in dignity.

Studies have shown that many behavioral differences, even in children, are biologically based. Male brains work in different ways than female brains. Certain academic strengths were given to the girls and others to boys. Communication skills seem to be distributed differently between the two sexes, as we see that it is sometimes easier to talk to and understand one of your own sex than it is to understand the other.

The differences between the boys and the girls are even more noticeable after puberty. Puberty is the stage of life after childhood, during which the boy begins to become a man and the girl begins to

A Unique Time for Growth

As young men and women, we begin to experience different feelings during this period of adolescence. We may feel awkward, self-conscious, confused or moody. Other feelings arise that increase our interest in the opposite sex, when just a few years ago we used to think they were "yucky". One day we may be insecure and the next day we may want independence. Sometimes we struggle for independence from our parents. Acting mature in spite of these feelings and changes is part of growing up. Our feelings and changes are not an excuse to act immaturely. It's a crucial time to continue our growth in character, so that our actions are not based on our fluctuating and unreliable feelings.

It is important to talk over these feelings and changes with our parents, since they have already been through adolescence and God has given them

become a woman. The growth from boy to man is at a different pace than the growth from girl to woman. She might mature sooner in a physical way; but when he catches up to her size, he will often pass her up, growing faster and taller a few years later.

During this growth time, he may be emotionally steady, while her moods are like a roller coaster from day to day. The guys often enjoy more aggressive activities like crashing into each other in football and wrestling. This is not as attractive to the girls, however, who might be more concerned than the boys with how their clothes and hair look. These growing differences are the beginning of the challenge to understand the opposite sex as we grow into adulthood and approach a possible marriage in the future. It is a time to look at the complementarity God placed in the male and female and think of how we can work together to serve God.

I give you thanks that I am fearfully, wonderfully made; wonderful are your works.

—Psalm 139:14 (New American Standard Bible)

the responsibility to help us through. The *Parent Guide* that accompanies this workbook is filled with information to help you and your parents discuss these issues of sexuality from a biological, emotional, intellectual, social and moral perspective.

Am I Normal?

All of these changes are normal, and they occur spontaneously in varying degrees and at different times in each of us—because each one of us is *unique,* and God has a special plan for our personal growth. Young teens are all at different stages of growth, so there is generally no need to worry about whether you are among the first or the last to grow. Within five years, most of your friends or classmates will be close to their adult size. Talking to your parents will help. They can let you know at what age some of the people in their family reached puberty, so you will know what to expect.

Solution Time

How can the two sexes, male and female, complement and harmonize one another's strengths and weaknesses in:

- Verbal communication skills? _____

_____

_____

- Working on a project together? _____

_____

_____

- Doing household chores? _____

_____

_____

- Running a family? _____

_____

_____

The Road to Adulthood

Our most important challenge during puberty is to grow **spiritually** while we are growing physically, so that we can express our sexuality in mature and responsible ways. Remember, human sexuality includes the physical, mental, social, emotional *and spiritual* traits that make you a man or woman. **What good would it be to have a physically mature body and be a spiritual baby who cannot make good moral choices?**

If you are healthy, you will most likely become physically sexually mature without exerting any conscious effort besides getting enough rest and eating a good diet. But—will you become sexually mature in all the other ways? That's up to you. It depends on whether you follow God's plan for sexuality and learn about real love, or whether you treat sexual beauty merely as something for physical gratification.

The physical changes of adolescence take place to fulfill God's plan for the complementarity of the sexes. Man and woman are designed physically and chemically different. As they mature, they learn to balance and harmonize their differences, picking up and sharing each other's strengths and supporting each other's weaknesses. Then they can learn to work together well.

The Two Become One

The physical complementarity of the sexes also takes on a special meaning because it encourages us to grow not only for each other, but also for society and for the future as well. God designed these differences to be oriented toward marriage and family life, even though all people are not called to the vocation of marriage.

The mature complementary nature of man and woman is a complex design of the Creator. Understanding the opposite sex takes many years of effort in working together at home, in school or at our jobs. Yet the male–female differences are all here for God's reasons. One of those reasons is to allow us to grow in the fullness of life; another is to bring children into the world in a family.

God in his wisdom gives us a source of His grace in the Sacrament of Matrimony for those couples whom He calls to join their lives together. This great grace helps men and women overcome the differences and challenges they face in the vocation of marriage.

SEX is God's wedding gift to you... no fair peeking!

Entering the Sacrament of Matrimony is a free choice. It is a covenant of love like God's covenant with His people, not just a brotherly love such as the love between you and your close friends. The covenant of love for married couples includes conjugal love, the unifying love of husband and wife in all facets of their sexuality; spiritual, emotional, social and physical. The covenant of married love is a union with God of two whole persons, not just two bodies. This is part of God's wonderful plan of life and love.

God gave married couples a special, holy assignment in marriage to unite their lives together. God assigned a man and woman to become one, to unify their complementary natures by becoming one in heart, mind and flesh. "Therefore a man leaves his father and his mother and cleaves to his wife, and they become one flesh" (Genesis 2:24).

God was also very clear that marriage is the only dignified place for this full conjugal union. How can we see this?

- *Man shall leave his father and mother.* In this biblical writing, the leaving is official. *Leave* means to leave legally and socially, not just go off somewhere for a few hours, weeks or years, but leave—start your own family, get a marriage license, take one family name, make the commitment official in front of the community.
- *Cleave [cling] to his wife.* Healthy, mature clinging involves love and devotion, a total giving of the inner self, pledging fidelity, and resisting separation. Pope John Paul II called it "self-donation", or a total gift of yourself to your spouse.
- *They become one flesh [one body].* If the man and woman are united sacramentally, spiritually, socially, emotionally and legally, they can then unite to become one flesh, that is, one body. They create one unified life together, and are open to creating new life with God.

Is there a different Bible that puts these things in reverse order? No. Well, according to worldly TV and movies, we first become one flesh, then let our relationship get really clingy in an immature manner—and then finally decide to get married, if at all. That's a huge contradiction of the Creator's plan, and it brings all types of problems into a relationship. God has assigned the sexual union as an expression of the marital union and not only in the Old Testament. Jesus repeated the order in Matthew 19:5 when He quotes Genesis 2:24 almost word for word. There is never a mention in Scripture or Church teaching of premarital union being permitted or being good. Premarital union, called fornication in the Scriptures, is spoken of only as "sin" and "evil" in the Bible. The Church didn't make this up, God did—and with good reason. He wants us to protect the dignity of love and life so we can fulfill His plan for us.

In marriage a man and woman express a total gift of themselves to one another in union with

"Truly you have formed my inmost being; you knit me in my mother's womb"

Psalm 139.13

God. In this mature state of selfless commitment, a man and a woman give total love through the heart, mind and body, and this love can live on through the next generation. Using one's sexual powers in marriage can be a beautiful way of serving God when it is a means of expressing total love and is open to giving life. It is within marriage that children have a safe environment. This parenting relationship thrives only on a mature notion of love and life. Love and life are inseparably linked because God's love gives life.

Procreation: A New Life Created in the Image of God

Melissa, a seventeen-year-old sexual morality student, spoke to other teens when she put the truth about sexuality in her own words:

> When God created man He called us to join Him in the continuance of the human race. This is a pretty special calling, so teens should know the correct and moral way to use this gift.

> This new human we can create from our love is a gift from God. So before bringing a child into the world, God first asks us to be part of the total

commitment of marriage. Some teens might think that just liking each other a lot or even having strong romantic feelings for each other is enough commitment to have a sexual union. Although some teens feel they are just as responsible as adults, if they are not responsible enough to be committed to a marriage, then they are certainly not ready to take on the responsibility that goes with the physical marital union.

God has not simply asked us to reproduce; He has asked us to join Him in procreation. Procreation is the loving choice of a husband and wife, as well as the creative powers of God, working together to extend God's family. When I realize that God has asked all married couples to join Him in creating another human being, it really makes me stop and think. I can help God in creating a new human being and all He asks me to do is wait until marriage.

The reason God asks us to have children inside a marriage is because of the importance of a child growing up in the right environment. It is also that God asks us to instruct His family about their God, His people and the beauty and dignity of their sexuality. So all of these things put together emphasize the importance of learning about our sexuality as we grow into Christian adults.

We were made in the image of God. We were made male and female. We were made to love as God loves. God forbids us to use our bodies for mere physical pleasure, ignoring the spiritual dimension and the grace of the Sacrament of Matrimony. We were not made to use others or to be used by others for physical pleasure. Our body is a temple of the Holy Spirit. We were made to love and be loved, and to give our lives to God and each other as we mirror the unconditional love of God.

A LIFE OF VIRTUE

Ready for Life?

God loves each of us in our uniqueness. God knew us before we were born. He created us in His image with dignity and worth. He wants us to share all eternity with Him, so He thought we were worth dying for. His love for us is not dependent on our looks, our clothes, our popularity or our social class. How wonderful it is to be loved unconditionally by God!

In order to have a happy life and a good relationship with God, Who loves us, we need to make this love a two-way street. Jesus tells us to love God with our whole heart, our whole soul, and our whole mind, as well as to love our neighbor as ourselves. "On these two commandments depend all the Law and the prophets" (Matthew 22:37-40). God knew that a life of love would not always be easy for us in our fallen human nature, so He instructs us in virtue. In His Fatherly love for us, at Baptism He

places in our hearts the theological virtues of faith, hope and love.

The moral virtues are the ones we have to work on with our human efforts and God's helping grace, until they become habits for us. The four cardinal virtues are prudence, justice, fortitude and temperance. They are the basis for the other human virtues.

A human virtue is a habit of doing good. Virtue is "beauty on the inside" of the person—the kind of beauty God looks at. Virtue is also the key to maintaining order in our lives. Some virtues we should be developing are honesty, patience and chastity. What other virtues can you think of?

———————————————————————————

———————————————————————————

———————————————————————————

If you haven't studied the virtues in religion class yet, you can read more about them in the *Catechism of the Catholic Church,* numbers 1803–1811.

It's one thing to know what is good and to value it. It's another thing to *practice* doing good and acting like the Image of God we were made to be. In our personal struggle to find happiness we are sometimes confused if we don't follow God's directions. After all, He made us! He knows our strengths and weaknesses. We might even need an action plan to train ourselves to grow in virtue, just as we train for sports or music. Maybe your parents or older brother or sister would help coach! As we learn more about ourselves in the teen years, we find out which virtues are easier for us, and which are more challenging for us. The challenging ones will take practice to master, but when we master them, we respect ourselves more.

Self-Knowledge Helps Us Live Better

God made us to be saints in progress. He knows our strengths and weaknesses, and He blesses our efforts with His grace. We need to know ourselves enough to face the truth about who we are, to accept the things we cannot change, and then work to change the things that we are able to improve.

Do you know people who you think are beautiful and popular, but who always put themselves down by saying, "I'm so ugly" or "No one likes me"? You wonder why they say such things when they appear to have so much going for them. Then you may also know people who think they are really good and important, but they are not living according to the plan of our Creator at all. You might wonder if they either don't know themselves, don't accept themselves or don't want to improve themselves.

God gives each person a different set of gifts and talents. It's each person's job to know and develop those gifts and talents so each of us can fulfill God's unique plan for us. When we live according to God's plan, we can find a much deeper joy than what mere popularity can bring. We also won't have to try to be like everyone else.

What if you don't like yourself because you're not pleasing God or obeying your parents? What if you feel as though you're in a rut? What if your life seems out of control? Then begin to **change! You can!** Sometimes we need drastic change, and sometimes we need gentle daily steps to be more virtuous people.

What a great gift God has given us in our ability to change. He never sticks us in a rut and tells us "You have to be this way forever." If you get yourself in a rut, He'll help you out. Even if you are wrapped up in sin and turn to Him for mercy, He will forgive you and lift you up with His grace. If you don't like one of your bad habits, like biting your nails or overeating, or one of your favorite sins—like criticizing others, putting on a fake personality or being lazy—ask God to help you order your life. Ask Him

to help you change your bad habits. Take small steps if you need to. Change from immature habits to more mature ones, one at a time.

Adolescence is an important time to get to know ourselves in the eyes of God and develop character, a life of virtue.

What are some of the gifts or talents God has given you?

_____

_____

_____

_____

You have special gifts and talents, and He wants you to develop them in a special way that only you can. What can you do to develop them?

_____

_____

_____

_____

If you put yourself down, you are insulting God and His creation. Be who you were meant to be! You can be His instrument of Christian love to the world. You owe your best efforts to God.

If you have trouble deciding, ask someone who knows you well to help point out your strengths. Other people can help us see ourselves.

Now take an inventory of your weaknesses. This is not necessarily a confession; it is a realistic look at yourself. Circle those that sometimes match you, and add others you may have:

Undisciplined	Scatterbrained
Bossy	Argumentative
Fussy	Impatient
Indecisive	Negative attitude
Inconsistent	Moody
Stubborn	Critical
Proud	Permissive
Withdrawn	Indifferent
Overly sensitive	Depressed
Worrier	Aimless
Angry	Resentful
Lazy	_____
Messy	_____
Show-off	

If you have trouble seeing your weaknesses, ask for help from a parent, close friend or sibling. Otherwise, take this list to God, privately in prayer. He will show you lovingly. Allow Him to speak to your heart, and let Him show you where you can improve a little at a time as you grow into maturity the next few years.

When you can admit and see those good qualities that do not come naturally to you, you can begin to work on improving yourself. You may be able to turn some of your negatives into positives. Remember what St. Peter and St. Paul did with their big mouths? They preached the Good News. Someone who is bossy could become a leader; someone who enjoys arguing could become a pro-life lawyer. Think of more examples. You can work with God's grace to shrink your weaknesses, grow your strengths and develop stronger character. God made us to be more like Him. We are happier when we improve ourselves each day.

Take an inventory of your strengths. Circle the ones that apply to you, and add others you may have:

Sociable	Brave
Adventurous	Diplomatic
Peaceful	Deep
Considerate	Cheerful
Spontaneous	Peacemaker
Reserved	Perfectionist
Respectful	Competitive
Patient	Listener
Optimistic	Talkative
Orderly	Persistent
Friendly	Intelligent
Confident	_____
Consistent	_____
Loyal	

Exercising Virtue

1. Look up number 2340 in the *Catechism*. What are the five means we need to adopt to remain faithful to our baptismal promises and resist temptations?

   _____

   _____

   _____

   _____

   _____

2. Which of these do I need to acquire first?

   _____

   _____

   _____

   _____

   _____

You may want to ask a friend or family member to do a similar plan for himself and you can hold one another accountable to your goals. Look back each month and see how you are doing. Once you have completed work on the top three, add new ones to your list.

Grow in Confidence by Growing in Character

Many of us go through a stage when we are not confident of ourselves. Some teens respond by verbally "putting down" themselves or others. Other teens respond to their insecurity by seeking popularity or attention. Real security is found not in what others say or think about us, but by living the way God commands us. Therefore, the real way to grow in confidence is to love God first and most, work to develop our strengths, diminish our weaknesses, and work to love and serve others. Growing in character and maturity will make it easier to practice all the virtues, especially chastity.

Grow in Love by Serving Others

One great way to learn about love is to serve others with a cheerful heart. This is why Confirmation classes and youth groups often give us a requirement to fulfill service hours. By acting like Christ, spending our lives for others (instead of only ourselves), we practice learning to love. Do you know the line in St. Francis's prayer, "It is in giving that we receive"? That's what happens when you give of your time and talents in Christian service. You receive from God feelings of satisfaction and fulfillment that are reminders that you are doing what you are meant to do. Giving of your time and talents to others is an important step in learning about real love for real life.

Acting in a way that puts others ahead of your selfish interests is what being mature is all about. People growing in maturity have a better chance of growing in the fullness of life and love.

Maturity

How much do you know about being mature? If the person in the example is acting maturely, put an **M** on the line in front of the statement; if immaturely, put an **I** on the line.

1. _____ "I'm sorry; I was wrong."
2. _____ "I can't wait for my little brother after school. I've got to get home to play baseball."
3. _____ "Dad, you look tired. Let me shine your shoes for you."
4. _____ "I'll think of a good excuse for breaking that window, so I don't get into trouble."
5. _____ "I'm good in art. I'll offer to make the banner for the class Mass."
6. _____ "I know I didn't take out the garbage again; I forgot!"
7. _____ "That rule about gum is stupid. I'll chew it anyway and try not to get caught."
8. _____ "I'll volunteer at the hospital. They need teen helpers on Saturdays."
9. _____ "I can't afford to give to the poor. I'm saving up for a new ten-speed bike."
10. _____ "I'll skip TV tonight so I can do a good job on this homework."
11. _____ "No, I'm not going to take some. That's stealing!"
12. _____ "I can't lie to my mother about where we're going. I'll just have to tell the other kids no."
13. _____ "I'll do the dishes for you."

God always loves you.
Grow in His image.

Practicing Virtue

The soccer player who doesn't practice has little to offer the coach or the team. Teens who are not practicing to grow in virtue have very little to offer God, or their future spouses if they get married later on. It's time to start learning and practicing now.

What virtues do you need to learn more about? What virtues do you need to grow in?

On the next page there is a chart to help you find out.

Each week during the next three months, select a different virtue from this list and try to grow in it. First define the virtue and ways to practice it. If you like, ask a parent or a friend to help you rate your progress.

VIRTUE	DEFINITION	WAYS TO PRACTICE IT	RATE MYSELF
Faith			
Hope			
Love			
Prudence			
Justice			
Fortitude			
Temperance			
Honesty			
Patience			
Chastity			
Obedience			
Humility			

A LIFE OF LOVE

Practice Makes Perfect

Building blocks to love and life include our practice of love in the families and friendships we have now. We were made to love God and to love others in the way that Christ loves us—unconditionally.

Let's look at real love—not the superficial one in the ads or the movies, but the real thing that we have to practice if we are to grow in spiritual maturity during our teen years. God commands us to love Him with our whole heart, soul, mind and will. He commands us to love our neighbor as ourselves. These were not just suggestions, remember, they were commands!

The central question for us is "How are we living out this love in our own lives?" Love is a decision of the will. Love is the willingness to sacrifice ourselves for the good of another person. We are trying to perfect our lives, but we are not automatically going to become great, selfless lovers of God just because it is our sixteenth birthday, our wedding, our ordination or because we are professing religious vows. We don't make the varsity basketball team just by showing up at the first game. It takes years of coaching, practice and team cooperation to become a good basketball player. Likewise, in order to become great lovers in our adult vocations, we must start practicing now, play by play, step by step.

The family that God gave each of us is our first school of love. It is the best place to start practicing unselfish love. We are old enough now to be helpful, to serve our families, to be understanding and to give moral support, care and concern. Christ taught us many things about love and life. He spent the first thirty years of His life in loving obedience to His

parents to show us the importance of family love and obedience.

Let's examine some of the traits of love. Since we were made to love, love should be the root of all of our relationships. This selfless love should be practiced in our friendships, our family interaction and our relationship with God Who made us. Without these forms of sacrificial love, sexual morality will not make sense. People who do not understand that life is for giving and sharing think that life is only for fun and pleasure. Love is not always fun, but it does bring joy. These quizzes will help us examine our practices of love.

Love Quiz 1: Loving Our Friends and Companions

Read I Corinthians 13:4-8 and privately check your progress in Christian love. In the right column, draw a heart (♥) if you already have acquired that loving quality, or a cross (†), if you are trying to progress in that area.

Are you patient? _____

Can you wait for others without complaining? _____

Do you avoid telling others their faults? _____

Can you turn frustration into prayer and understanding? _____

Are you kind? _____

Do you avoid gossip? _____

Do you care about other people's feelings? _____

Are you thoughtful of other's needs before they ask? _____

Do you share your time generously? _____

Do you keep from jealousy or possessiveness? _____

Do you avoid trying to control others for your gain? _____

Do you keep from being snobbish? _____

Are you nice to people you do not know? _____

Do you treat others as Christ would? _____

Are you warm and sympathetic? _____

Do you keep from rudeness, always displaying good manners? _____

Do you carry a gloomy cloud around you? _____

Do you tease or annoy others? _____

Do you keep from selfishness and demanding your own way? _____

Are you too touchy and sensitive? _____

Do you control your anger? _____

Do you pray for others when tempted to be angry? _____

Do you keep from holding grudges? _____

Are you quick to forgive? _____

Do you keep from rejoicing when someone does wrong? _____

Do you avoid saying "I told you so"? _____

Do you think the best of others? _____

Do you rejoice when good wins out? _____

Do you help others along when they are struggling? _____

Are you trustworthy? _____

Are you positive and hopeful? _____

Are you dependable? _____

Are you quick to show sorrow after offending others? _____

Look over the areas where you love well, and those where you could improve. Your confessor, parents or a close friend may be able to help you with your struggles. Thank God for giving you His grace. Develop new habits to improve a little each day from now till the end of your life.

> Blessed are those who give without remembering and receive without forgetting.

Love Quiz 2: Loving My Family

Rate yourself as a contributing family member.

	4 always	3 usually	2 sometimes	0 never
Give good example to brothers or sisters				
Cheerfully respond to parents' requests				
Promptly obey				
Am always honest				
Am kind to brothers and sisters				
Clean my room and do chores				
Volunteer for extra chores				
Apologize when I've hurt someone				
Tell others I appreciate them				
Accept discipline without sulking				
Help with expenses				
Forgive others when they offend me				
Console others when they're down				
Compliment parents				
Phone home when I'll be late				
Do errands cheerfully				
Care for younger family members				
Bring friends home to meet my family				
Pray for parents				
Smile				
Spend time with parents and ask advice in serious matters				
Discuss differences calmly				
Tell parents where I go				
Share with family members				

Add your score and rate yourself. Then take a few moments to reflect and share your thoughts in a prayer with Jesus.

85–100 excellent
75–84 superior
60–74 good
40–59 fair
0–39 pray for help

PRAYER FOR PEACE

Lord, make me an instrument of your peace!
   Where there is hatred, let me sow love;
   where there is injury, pardon;
   where there is doubt, faith;
where there is despair, hope;
   where there is darkness, light;
   and where there is sadness, joy.

O Divine Master, grant that I may not so much seek
   to be consoled as to console;
   to be understood as to understand;
   to be loved as to love;
   for it is in giving that we receive;
   it is in pardoning that we are pardoned;
   and it is in dying that we are born to eternal life.

—Saint Francis of Assisi

Love Quiz 3: Practicing the Right Things to Say

In the left column is an unloving response that may be heard in some families. In the blanks on the right, fill in a loving response you could substitute.

1. "It's your job and your turn!" _____
2. "Sorry, I don't have time!" _____
3. "Stay away from my room!" _____
4. "Don't do it that way!" _____
5. "Is that the best you can do?" _____
6. "Shut up!" _____
7. "Why should I?" _____
8. "You never pick me up on time!" _____
9. "You never listen to me!" _____
10. "Were you born that way?" _____
11. "I don't feel like it!" _____
12. "None of your business!" _____
13. "It's not my fault!" _____

Write the loving phrases you wish to practice saying more often this week:

_____

_____

_____

_____

Love Quiz 4: Love for God

Answer yes or no to these questions:

- Do I remember to pray morning, noon and night? _____
- Do I really try to "lift up my mind and heart to God" during my prayers? _____
- Do I try my best to concentrate during Mass on praising and listening to God? _____
- Do I talk to Jesus as my friend and companion throughout the day? _____
- Do I join my sufferings to Christ on the cross? _____
- Do I express sorrow for my venial sins by going to confession as often as I need to? _____
- Do I try to avoid any thought, word or deed that offends God? _____
- Do I praise God and thank God and not just ask Him for what I want? _____
- Do I try to learn and live the will of God for my life? _____
- Do I try to increase my love for God with my whole heart, soul, mind and will? _____

Our personal relationship with God will be the foundation of our ability to love. Our love for God should be the motive to live all the virtues. Our love of God is what makes us sorry for our sins. The moral life is our response to God's great love for us.

Well, how are you doing? It takes a lifetime to perfect this love, but start trying now and you may surprise yourself. Come back to this chapter each month and check your progress. Become a better lover, step by step. Remember that you are not alone. Christ is always there to help you. Actually, He's waiting to hear from you all the time, and He wants you to ask for His help. Stay close to Him as you learn to love. The more Christ lives in you, the more charitable you will be to others, too!

A LIFE OF FRIENDSHIP

We all need friends. While having fun in the process, friends can help each other become better people. God wants us to have friends and to be a friend. Remember He even said "It is not good that the man should be alone" (Genesis 2:18). Friendship is an important part of love and life. Our friendships during adolescence can help prepare us for married love or celibate love.

Friends divide our sorrow and multiply our joy. A true friend is more than just another person on our sports team or in our class. A friend is someone who cares about you and always wants the best for you. Friends are our companions in life who give us a chance to practice listening, kindness, patience and understanding. A good friend can help us see ourselves as we really are. A friend is someone we can just be with; friends are comfortable in each other's presence. Good friendships take time and care to develop. To have a friend, you must be a friend.

As one reaches adolescence, friendships can grow deeper, so it's important to choose your friends wisely. The qualities we look for in a friend are some of the same ones we're trying to develop in ourselves:

Respect	Positive attitude
Consideration	Generosity
Trust	Sense of humor
Loyalty	Honesty

What else do you look for in a friend?

_____ _____

_____ _____

In the Old Testament Book of Sirach, the Word of God teaches us about friendships. Read Sirach 6:5–17 and then answer the following questions:

1. What is God's advice on how to multiply your number of friends? _____

_____

_____

2. Should your confidants be many or few?_____

3. What should you do to be cautious when you make a new friend? _____

_____

_____

4. What are the some ways friends can be unfaithful?_____

_____

_____

5. What are the four descriptions of a "faithful" friend in the later verses?_____

_____

_____

6. Why is a faithful friend such a treasure?

_____

_____

_____

7. Why is it important to have friends who are reverent and obedient to God? _____

_____

_____

_____

Friends are to be loved. They are not to be *used* for popularity, status, money or other selfish purposes.

An important consideration in choosing friends and companions is whether they strive to do what is right. People who are not trying to live a moral life are more likely to give in to evil inclinations. They

1. Does my friend bring out the worst in me or the best in me?_____

2. Am I a better Christian because of our friendship?_____

3. Do we waste our time together or spend our time together well?_____

4. Do we spend a lot of time complaining and criticizing?_____

5. Do I feel happy to be around this person?_____

6. Do my parents like my friend?_____

7. Is my friend's behavior respectful?_____

8. Are we really good friends or just casual acquaintances?_____

9. Does this person bring more problems to my life or more solutions?_____

10. Can we have good, clean fun together and avoid temptation?_____

will be prone to many kinds of sins: ridiculing others, bullying, shoplifting, lying, drinking, smoking, abusing drugs or seeking power in gangs or violence. These behaviors that some teens choose are never truly satisfying, and they are all destructive.

Pope John Paul II spoke to youth directly on this: "In times of darkness, do not seek escape. Have courage to resist the dealers in deception who make capital of your hunger for happiness and who make you pay dearly for a moment of artificial paradise—a whiff of smoke, a bout of drinking or drugs. What claims to be a shortcut to happiness leads to nowhere."

Drugs and alcohol can only cause you to lose control so that you will not be able to make good moral choices. The friends and companions we choose should be a positive influence on our lives, and we should try to be a good influence on theirs.

Friends are the people with whom we will share many of our joys and sorrows. Preparing ourselves for mature love involves learning how to be a great friend by listening, advising, asking, sharing and praying—not using or being used.

Here are questions that can help you evaluate the quality of your friendships. Think of your closest friend and answer the questions with him or her in mind.

FRIENDSHIP
A friend is like a tower strong.
A friend is like a joyous song
   That helps us on our way.
When golden ties of friendship bind
The heart to heart, the mind to mind,
   How fortunate are we!
For friendship is a noble thing:
It soars past death on angel's wing
   Into eternity.
God blesses friendship's holy bond
Both here and in the great beyond;
   A benefit unpriced.
Then may we know that wondrous joy,
That precious ore without alloy;
   A friendship based on Christ.

Planning your time with your friends will make your time together more enjoyable. Unplanned evenings with friends or dates usually lead nowhere. It is so boring to hear these conversations:

"What do you want to do?"
"I don't know; what do you want to do?"
"I don't care; you decide."
"I don't care either; you decide."

Someone (you!) must take the initiative and make some plans. Idleness usually leads to trouble. If there is really nothing to do, *stay home.* Try some of the following ideas to make fun happen. Life is too short to waste time!

What to Do with Your Friends That Can Be Fun and Fulfilling

Time spent with friends can be fun and fulfilling if you use that great imagination God gave you and plan ahead. Here are some suggestions to get you started.

- Plan to break some Guinness World Records.
- Make your own pizza from scratch. (It will take time.) Start with the yeast, water and flour. (Make sure to clean up afterward.)

- Borrow or rent a video camera and make a movie or TV show with a good message to play for someone's little brothers or sisters.
- Attend local sports events.
- Prepare and serve a seven-course gourmet meal.
- Play Monopoly and learn how others react to greed, chance, disappointment, fate, wealth or poverty.
- Play charades and really test your communication skills.
- Attend your local community or high school plays.
- Go to Mass or to confession on Saturday afternoon.
- Play tennis, miniature golf or ping-pong.
- Have a joke and riddle party—each person must come prepared with three jokes or riddles that are clean and decent. Laugh together!
- Complete a paint-by-number canvas.
- Attend a *good* concert. (Classical music has been around for hundreds of years— there must be something to it.)
- Ride bicycles.
- Go boating, bowling, skiing or fishing (plenty of time to converse).
- Try sledding, ice skating or snowball fighting in the winter.
- Do your homework together.

- Anonymously shovel people's sidewalks on a snowy night.
- Visit the elderly, lonely or sick. Offer to do an errand for the person, or bring a treat to share (be sure to find out first if the person is on a restricted diet).
- Make soft pretzels at home. This takes strength (for kneading), patience (for rising) and coordination (for shaping).
- Don't forget "Trivial Pursuit".
- Make and decorate a birthday cake, bring it to a nursing home and give it to the person with the nearest birthday. Create a smile!
- Put on a play for your neighborhood.
- Wash your family car.
- Make your own art exhibit.
- Do some painting or maintenance for your grandparents.
- Go on a picnic or have a barbecue in the yard.
- Play an encyclopedia game to help increase your knowledge.
- Clean the garage.

- Show old movies (like *It's a Wonderful Life*) on the VCR or DVD.
- Plan your family's menus and do the grocery shopping for the week. (So you'll get the food you like.)
- Play some of the older board games you may have in your house.
- Throw a "theme" costume party and have everyone come dressed as historical (or hysterical), cartoon or biblical characters.
- Look for a need you can fill.
- Read the Bible together and discuss it. Start with the Book of Proverbs or Wisdom or Sirach and pick out your favorite advice for living.

Keeping your life busy and full of doing good will help you adjust to many of the changes that are occurring in your life right now. Some of the feelings that are surfacing may seem confusing and have the potential to be destructive. If they are put into per-

spective and channeled into constructive, creative activities, however, these drives will be sources of growth in your life.

List five other creative things to do:

1. _____

2. _____

3. _____

4. _____

5. _____

Discussion Time:

Take time to talk about friendships with your parents, grandparents and peers and see what the different generations have to say about these questions:

1. What do you think of the following quote? "It is better to have no friends at all, than friends who will lead you to Hell?"
2. What can a teen do to practice the courage needed to separate from a destructive relationship? What can he do about the loneliness he might feel afterward?
3. Think of some examples of loyal and good friends that you may have read about or seen in film or on TV. What qualities of friendship can you learn from these characters?
4. How can friends help us become better people?
5. How can you help your friends become better people?
6. Read and discuss the Bible passage in the Book of Wisdom, chapter 4, verses 10–15. What slowly happens to a good person who hangs around with people who are fascinated with evil?

A LIFE OF EMOTIONAL MATURITY

Emotionally Yours

"I did it because I *felt* like it."

Is that an emotionally mature or immature statement? *Feelings* are the roller coasters of life—so much depends on how you ride them. How do you stay on track?

Mature people ride their emotions in this way: first they feel, then they think, and finally they act. Emotionally immature people feel first, and then immediately act on their feelings. This type of immaturity is sometimes called impulsiveness. To "buckle up for safety", let's look at the road to self-control over our emotions.

Feelings Happen; Behavior Is a Choice

Babies, kids, teenagers and grownups all have feelings. As you mature physically during the teen years, you also have to mature emotionally. Emotional maturity requires self-control, so it takes human effort on our part. If you mature physically faster than you mature emotionally, you can become "out of balance" or emotionally unstable. This instability can happen often during adolescence, but with some effort, you can outgrow most of it before adulthood.

Emotionally immature people cannot tell the difference between their emotions and their thoughts, between what they feel and what they think. They do whatever they feel like doing, without caring how it will affect their own future and their eternal life. They don't care whether their actions will hurt other people. Another sign of emotional immaturity is to bury your feelings instead of working through them in a good way. Burying feelings, instead of expressing them in a healthy way, can lead to emotional or physical illness.

It is never too late for you to prevent this kind of emotional instability by building the muscles of your emotional maturity. An emotionally mature person knows that emotions are not equipped to make judgments; emotions are feelings without brains. Feelings just help to provide information about an experience. Emotions are used like a thermostat to register reactions to pleasure and pain. Emotions are reactions to our experiences so we can make judgments with our minds and act according to our will. An emotionally mature person can stop to think, calm down, use his mind, join with God in prayer, and work through a decision. Just like exercising a physical muscle, each time you act in an emotionally self-controlled manner, you are building your emotional maturity.

Emotional Freedom or Slavery?

Have you ever felt so mad at your brother that you could have killed him? Thank God you did not act on that! That emotion was only momentary, and some day your brother may be your best friend. Think of the other effects of living according to your emotions. If you feel mad at someone, should you throw a pair of scissors at him? If your teacher got angry with your class, should she give the whole class a failing grade? If you were jealous of someone, should you say bad things about her behind her back to make others dislike her?

There is no freedom in acting according to your feelings. Emotions serve their purpose by helping you prod your mind for a solution to the problem presented, but it is harmful to let your emotions drive your behavior. That would only make you a slave to your emotions.

Pleasure and Pain

An emotionally mature person can enjoy all the pleasure that is good for him and avoid pleasures that are harmful to him. An emotionally mature person can also accept all the pain that is good for him and reject all that is bad. Think of *pleasures* that are *good* for you, such as the satisfaction of finishing a big school project, the freedom of taking a bike ride in the park in spring, the warmth of sipping a hot drink after coming in from the snow, the closeness of having a long conversation with a friend who understands, the joy of getting a hug from your little brother or sister, the thrill of winning a game or a race, and so on.

On the other hand, some *pleasures* are *bad* for you. For example, winning an eating or drinking contest; teasing people until they hurt; putting poisons in your body by smoking or abusing drugs or alcohol; getting your own way all the time; putting down another person. These are pleasures that lead to no good. Of course, you can obviously name *pains* that are *bad* for you—like breaking a bone, being beaten up, having a friend betray you, flunking a test, or being made fun of by classmates. There are also *pains* that are *good* for you, such as a long sweaty workout before a championship game, skipping a movie with your friends in order to spend time with your little brother or sister, or taking a punishment when you know you deserve it. Also, you can have the good pain of humbling yourself to go to frequent confession. In fact, even guilt can be good for you if it reminds you that you are weak before God and must seek His mercy and grace through Reconciliation.

God created your senses to cause the reactions of your emotions. Your emotions were not created to tempt you, but to inform you. Emotionally mature people listen to their emotions but act based on what they **should do,** not what they **feel like doing.** Emotionally mature people try to live in a way that reflects the image in which they were made: the image of God.

This does not mean that emotions should be confused with conscience. Conscience makes moral judgments about the goodness or badness of something. A loving relationship with God through the sacraments and daily prayer and meditation can help you examine your conscience. Your study of religion and your parents' discipline can help you know the difference between the good pleasures and the bad pleasures, between the bad pains and the good or virtuous ones.

The Road to Emotional Maturity

Think about how you are doing on the road to emotional maturity. First, are you on the road at all? Are you aware that emotional maturity takes some practice? Do you know that Christ has redeemed all the parts of your personality, including your emotions? Do you ask Christ for the grace to grow in your emotional maturity and self-control?

When emotions are allowed to dominate, positively or negatively, people become unhappy. In their misery, they often cannot cope with the realities of life, so they find forms of escape like hedonism (pleasure seeking), alcohol abuse to "drown" their feelings, overeating, verbal abuse, bullying, violence, overworking, and so on. People who live by their emotions often contradict themselves from day to day. They are hard to live with and hard to understand. They have a hard time understanding themselves! Christ has called you to be more than that. You are to be apostles of His love. As you have already learned, love is much more than a feeling.

On the other hand, emotions should not be buried, either. There is nothing wrong with getting very excited about something good, or getting anxious about a big event coming up. Sometimes your emotions can motivate you to do good; **pleased, joyful, peaceful, hopeful, encouraged, excited, compassionate, generous, concerned,** and **tender** are some positive emotions that lead you to do good.

Angry, sad, disgusted, anxious, threatened, depressed, resentful, defiant, lonely and **lost** are some of the negative emotions you sometimes might feel. What are these feelings telling you? That something is wrong; that there is a problem to be solved; or that a danger is to be avoided? Then, do your best to try to solve the problem or avoid the danger. Maybe anger alerts you that someone is treating you unkindly. Pray harder, and try to find a peaceful solution. Don't use negative emotions as an excuse for bad behavior. Think. What would Jesus do? If your answer is "I don't know", you can learn more. Try reading a page of the New Testament each day until you get to know Him better.

Think about a time when you felt strong emotions. Were you able to behave as a Christian even in spite of or according to your feelings? In the following exercise, select four of the feelings listed above. In the second column, describe a Christian action that might be a proper response to that feeling.

	FEELING	CHRISTIAN RESPONSE
Example A	Anger	Forgiveness
Example B	Pleased	Do a favor for someone else

1. _____
2. _____
3. _____
4. _____

In order truly to love, you must be able to live with your emotions and use your intellect, will and well-formed conscience to decide how you are to think, speak and act as a Christian. Having your emotional life in order is a key to success in relationships with your family, your friends, and even with God!

New Feelings to Master

The changes that take place in you during adolescence include some new emotions that go along

with your growing physical maturity as men or women. One is a feeling of attraction to the opposite sex, and another is the romantic attachment to a person. Sometimes these feelings can take you by surprise. At other times you dream ahead and long for them. A teen who has already developed a healthy pattern of dealing with regular human emotions will not have a dramatic problem with the new emotions, because he has already practiced feeling, thinking about it, and acting according to what he knows he should do. The teen who spent his childhood using temper tantrums and manipulation on his parents may have more of a problem with these new emotions.

These new sexual feelings can be good for you if you do not let them dominate your behavior. For example, the feeling of attraction to the opposite sex can make a young teen take more interest in looking nice, brushing his teeth without his parents nagging him anymore, combing his hair and being kinder to others. A feeling of a secret attraction to a teacher might make a teen study harder in that subject. To use these new feelings well, we should not try to "act out" to get attention, whether in front of teens or adults. Sometimes feelings can go away by themselves, or be replaced by newer feelings. All feelings do not have to be acted upon.

A teen who is in the driver's seat of his emotions can adjust to the sexual feelings of adolescence without being dominated by them, being afraid of them, or without exploiting them for all the pleasure he can get.

The feeling of romantic attraction is one of the high points of emotional life. Great literature, music, drama and poetry are full of examples of the creativity that can be expressed when the feeling of romantic attachment is experienced. Romantic feelings will come and go in life, but usually with many memories attached. Romance is a feeling of the moment, an awesome feeling that can lead you to love. But it should not be exploited for your pleasure, or confused with love.

Although romantic feelings are great, they are overrated when people use them to determine the value of a relationship. If you are dancing with someone and you feel overwhelmed by a warm romantic feeling, it does not mean that you are in love. It means you are dancing so closely that you are causing a hormonal reaction . . . and you might want to take a step back!

Romantic feelings should never drive someone to commit a sexual sin, and they should not be the main reason for marriage. Some television shows improperly teach you that romantic feelings lead couples to go to bed together. Other sources teach you that romance is the primary reason to get married. These are lies because they leave out the *person* in a personal relationship. Each person is made of mind and will, of his past, present and future. It is such personal qualities of both people that are essential to developing a deep, loving relationship—far beyond just romantic feelings. When marriage is based only on feelings, or a sexual relationship exists outside the Sacrament of Matrimony, the relationship eventually becomes a curse rather than a blessing.

When watching a romance going wrong on television or in the movies, the audience can usually spot when a character is making a mistake. People in the audience may start thinking things such as, "No, stop! Can't you see that person is wrong for you? How could you be so stupid?" Oftentimes however, those same people in the audience who in their minds are shouting out against the character may be making the same mistake in their own lives. From the inside of a powerful romantic attachment, you can have a much harder time listening to logic. You can be blind to what is really going on—romantic feelings are that powerful! That's what people mean when they say love is blind. Romance might be blind, but real love is never blind.

Romantic feelings during the teen years can really harm you:

- If you allow yourself to get emotionally attached at too young an age
- If you attach yourself to a person who is not good for you
- If you hang out with someone who leads you into temptation
- If you stay with a person who creates a desire in you to steal the sexual pleasures that should be awakened only in marriage

That is why it is important to avoid those emotional and sexual attachments, and to prevent blindness by heeding the words of your friends and family if they warn you against such relationships.

Romantic feelings during the teen years do not need to be completely restrained. These feelings can be used for good when they help you to become better people for Christ. Romance can lead you out of yourself, away from your childish self-centeredness. Romance helps you to learn to think of others first. It helps bring out your best qualities as you try to show your better self.

Attraction or Lust?

Besides the feelings of attraction and romance, teens may experience an inner drive for sexual union. Due to their hormonal make-up, this is sometimes more difficult to handle for boys than girls. A young man's physical development is often ahead of his emotional development. He sees a girl who is beautiful and experiences the emotion of attraction, which can move quickly to sexual desire. He has a choice of what to think and do.

A Christian young man will train his mind to turn away from the temptation of feeding his sexual

desires. He will take a deep breath, retract his imagination, and thank God for the beauty He has placed in the world, particularly in that young woman before him. By turning his thoughts toward God and gratitude, he can avoid the sin of lust. Some young men will need to turn their thoughts to an entirely different subject, like sports or their favorite video game, to distract themselves. Those initial thoughts or feelings are not sins; they are thoughts or feelings that need to be channeled in order not to lead you into temptation.

A Christian young woman should dress and act in such a way that helps the young men see her as a person, not as a sexy object. Young Christian men will then notice these beautiful young women as persons who are loved by God, who should be respected in thoughts as well as words and deeds. Both young men and young women should avoid impure movies and websites, or immodest magazines, advertisements, and so forth.

Infatuation or Manipulation?

Another early feeling that comes with adolescent growth is infatuation, which is "being in love with love." This usually affects the girls sooner than the boys, because girls' sexual emotions awaken earlier than boys'. A young woman may desire love and fantasize about romance, finding a male friend, teacher or celebrity to help feed this fantasy. This is not a problem itself, since dreaming about being a future bride or being in the arms of Prince Charming are wonderful dreams. The problem comes if she chooses to act on her emotional attraction and it keeps her away from her daily work or prayers. She is especially off track if she "falls" for a boy who is willing to give her attention, even though he has very little character or self-control. If a young woman tries dressing

immodestly to get a boy's attention, she is leading both of them into temptation. If she is young and knows that marriage is still too far away, she is wasting her time playing games. From the beginning girls should resist the temptation of trying to manipulate men, so as not to become obnoxious and needful of the wrong kind of attention.

Called to Love

As you develop your ability to love others the way that Christ loves, you must learn to develop your loving capacity in all parts of your personality: *emotionally, intellectually, spiritually,* and *socially.* That means you have a lot of skills to learn over the next few years before adulthood. Being mature on each of these four levels will prepare you well to hear God's call, to receive your mission, your vocation. If your vocation is to marriage, God will bless you with permission after the wedding to develop your full capacity to love and be open to new life. If God calls you to the priesthood, or consecrated religious life, God will bless you with the freedom of celibacy to give and share your spiritual life with so many others. Each of these vocations requires your emotional maturity.

Emotional maturity will not be easy to attain, and it may take some time to develop. This is part of the self-mastery we need to be a truly loving person. If you find that you are riding this roller coaster of emotional life incorrectly, you can return to Christ in prayer and Reconciliation for the help He promises. Develop a special devotion to St. Joseph, the husband of the Blessed Virgin Mary. Joseph was able to love Mary in a chaste way, to care for her and Jesus, and to be a perfect model of manhood. Continue to foster a special relationship to the Blessed Virgin Mary, who was open only to God's will for her life, displaying beautiful traits of goodness, feminine strength, joy, humility and kindness.

PUT YOURSELF IN THE DRIVER'S SEAT — WITH SELF-MASTERY!

Many of you can hardly wait until you can get your driver's license and drive! But suppose that cars and driving were outlawed just before your sixteenth birthday. Someone persuaded Congress that driving was too dangerous, that drivers sometimes lose control, that lives are lost, that people drink and drive, that some drive without a license, that cars burn too much fuel and so on. So they're out! No more cars. No more driving.

"But wait," you argue, "cars are necessary! People have to drive to work, to hospitals, to the grocery store! C'mon! Most people on the road have their licenses; they stay within the speed limit and follow the rules. Most people can keep their cars under control."

You are right, of course. And cars will not be banned as long as people can keep them under control. The sex drive also needs to be controlled, and it also must be used according to rules. It is powerful and can be life supportive or life destructive. The sexuality advertised in our "arousing" culture is way out of bounds with what God established as natural and good. Sexual advertising is out of control. It is life destructive, just like a driver who is out of control.

In God's design we are each given a free will. We are not forced to please God like a puppet on a string. We choose to love Him freely, just as He chose to create us to live and love in His world. Our commitment of love for God works in the same way as God's commitment of love for us. We choose to love God, ourselves and others. This way of loving is vastly different from that of the lower animals. Animals operate only by instinct, not by choice.

God does not abandon us after He gives us the freedom to choose. He also offers His grace to help us to be good. Through prayer and the sacraments, we can receive the graces necessary to live good lives.

In God's design, there are two purposes for the marital act:

- To bring children into the world
- To unite spouses in ever-deepening love by renewing their marriage commitment

HOW ARE SEXUAL RELATIONS LIKE DRIVING? YOU NEED A LICENSE FOR BOTH!

> Dear St. Joseph, Head of the Holy Family, intercede for me. Help me to be pure in my thoughts, my words, and my deeds.
>
> Help me to be strong so I can live a life that leads me to goodness and obedience to God. You were so good at this; you were so strong. St. Joseph, you protected Mary and Jesus from harm. You were so close to God that you could hear His messages in your heart. Help me to do my part to be a blessing to my family, especially now during the teen years. Amen.

The Best Things in Life Are Worth Waiting For

You probably appreciate those things for which you have waited the longest. A spoiled child who gets a present every day in December will not be thrilled by a present on Christmas Day. It takes more and more to make him happy. People who use sexual activity as a tool for gratification will try to get what they want, when they want it. They haven't developed the virtue of patience or chastity, and they don't practice waiting. It takes more and more and different types of "thrills" for such people to satisfy their sexual appetite. They are never satisfied and soon become bored. They destroy what would have been a good experience in marriage, had they followed God's plan.

People who wait until marriage for sexual union can better appreciate and enjoy sexual expression. Their desire will be greater, and their joy will be deeper. God provides this satisfaction and joy for doing His will. In God's plan, sexual expression is sacred and holy for married couples. The pleasure is God's gift, not the goal.

It is also important to realize that though sexual drives can be good when ordered to the good of marriage, they are not desires for things we need. An individual cannot live without food, water and air. Those are needs, so our desires for those things must be fulfilled in order to sustain our lives. But sexual desires

Most lower animals take little responsibility for their offspring. The young animals live by their instincts, and these instincts are very strong.

We humans are much different. We must learn to love, to make good decisions, to accept responsibility and to control our desires. Human parents work many years to assure the proper growth of their children.

God created sexual desire. It is a good gift. He gave us this gift so that we will be able to express our love and commitment to our marriage partners and cooperate with God in the creation of new human beings, who in turn will themselves learn to know and love God.

Just as man fell into original sin, many men and women fall to sexual sin. The influences of the culture ignore the fact that God has redeemed all of us and offers the grace for us to live and love as He does. People who ignore the redemption and refuse the grace of God might struggle constantly with sexual temptations. The virtue of chastity—the spiritual energy that keeps our love from selfishness and aggressiveness—is a fruit of living with God the Holy Spirit inside of us.

> Chastity is the best,
> forget the rest.
> Be proud.
> And don't join the crowd because
> there's no room for mistakes,
> when once is all it takes.
> So when the time comes
> don't be bums.
> Say no thanks
> because you know what it takes.
>
> —Jim

are not a matter of life and death. **No one in history has ever died because of sexual abstinence.** The reproductive system is the only one that you don't have to use while living a long, healthy life. Yes, the sexual drive is a naturally good gift; but it needs to be controlled and used according to God's design. We can control our desires through the wise use of our minds and will power and with the helping grace of God. We can use our own wills to choose to do things in accordance with God's will.

Unlike animals, we are not slaves to our biology. We are persons made in the image of God. While we are on earth, our bodies should serve God and other people. Then we will be glorified in heaven after the Last Judgment, just as Christ's body is glorified in Heaven now. Our bodies help us to fulfill our purpose in life, which is to love God and to love others as we do ourselves. The sexual drive, which is a dimension of our bodies, should be used in selfless and life-supportive ways. It is not for us to abuse in selfish and life-destructive ways.

There are many ways in which we can use our bodies to help and serve others. Some are obvious, like helping your friend lift a heavy package or performing a ballet for the pleasure of an audience. Being a good listener is another, less obvious, way that we use our bodies. It requires our ears, our eyes, our facial expressions and, if our friend needs a hug or a high-five, our whole bodies!

List other ways we use our bodies to help our family members and friends in ways that glorify God:

At home: _____
With a musical instrument: _____
For a sports team: _____

> God didn't forbid sex before marriage because He wanted to watch us sweat it out. God doesn't treat us along the lines of sex like the fellow who starved his dog for a week and then put a juicy bone in front of him while telling him to "stay". God is not a celestial party pooper or a cosmic killjoy looking over the balcony of Heaven and yelling, "Stop that!" at people having a good time. God desires sex to be enjoyable in the framework of marriage. He is our protector and guide. He knows that in pre-marital intercourse, there is not the proper atmosphere necessary for pleasurable sexual intimacy. This atmosphere comes only from the lifetime commitment of marriage.
>
> —Les John Christie, *Dating and Waiting*, (Cincinnati, Ohio: Standard Publishing Company).

Activity Time

1. Look up Romans 13:14 and write the message here. _____
2. Write your own skit:
   a. Write a short skit or dialogue on a situation involving peer pressure to do something-wrong. Give at least one of the people in your skit a strong character that leads the others to do good. Make this character an example for other teens.
   b. Act out your skits for the group, or perform them for some younger students.

THE BUILDING BLOCKS
OF LOVE AND LIFE

What Do You Remember?

PART I. MATCHING—Put the letter of the missing word in the blanks below.
(2 pts. each)

A. chastity
B. God
C. sacrifice
D. virtue
E. friendship
F. fornication
G. marriage
H. think

1. Emotionally mature people _____ before they act.
2. The situation in which sexual union is good and holy is _____.
3. Love is willingness to _____ oneself for the good of another person.
4. The word used in the Bible for premarital sex or sexual sin is _____.
5. A relationship between two or more people who have common interests, who are helping each other grow in Christian maturity is called _____.
6. A _____ is the habit of doing good.
7. _____ is the virtue that moderates our sexual desires according to God's design; sexual self-control; a spiritual energy that helps us love properly.
8. Human beings are created to reflect the image of _____.

PART II. FILL IN THE BLANK OR BLANKS with the correct word or phrase to complete the meaning of the sentence. Here are the answer choices for Part II; some words may be used more than once.

family	lovers
gifts	God
mind	heart
yourself	choose
control	plan
soul	feelings
complement	dignity

1. God created man and woman to complete and _____ one another, because He saw that it wasn't good for man to be alone.

2. People who make decisions based only on their _____ need to grow in emotional maturity.

3. Male and female, though made differently, are equal in
_____.

4. The two greatest commandments: (a) Love God with your
whole_____, _____ and
_____, and (b) Love your neighbor as
_____.

5. Our dignity and worth as human beings comes from
_____, Who is Love.

6. God wants us to develop our _____ and talents to
the best of our ability for His glory and our happiness.

7. An important key to having fun together is to _____
your activities ahead of time.

8. It's important to practice and develop self-_____
daily, so we will be strong to resist when tempted.

9. God has given us a mind and free will so we are not forced to love Him,
but can _____ to love Him freely.

10. We must be great _____, just as Jesus was.

PARENT–TEEN DISCUSSION

Teens who want to be mature must take time to look at themselves as well as their relationships with others. Let's start with our relationships at home. Do we ever think about our parents and what they're going through?

Here is an opportunity to do so. Answer the following questions and discuss them with your parents. They have a corresponding questionnaire in their *Parent Guide*.

For Teens Only: How Well Do You Know Your Parents?

1. What makes your mom or dad most happy?_____
2. What is her or his greatest aggravation? _____
3. Circle the words that best describe your parents:

    peaceful   cheerful   busy   content   moody   helpful   anxious

4. What is causing your parents the greatest concern right now?

    money   job   children   marriage   health of a family member

5. Parents of teens have a big job to teach responsibility, self-control, decision making and mature love. Check the ways your parents have been guiding you to learn these things?
    _____ by their example
    _____ by having you clean your own room
    _____ by asking your help with household chores
    _____ by letting you buy some things for yourself
    _____ by teaching you to do your own laundry
    _____ by being kind to family members
    _____ by helping you take responsibility for your
        own decisions and their consequences
    _____ by fostering forgiveness among family members
    _____ other:_____

6. What can we do to help each other learn more about love and life?

    _____

    _____

    _____

THE GREAT RACE

After seeing the great gifts that God has given to us, we naturally want to return that love in the best way possible. To do this, we must turn toward Christ and make Him the goal of our lives, the end of our great race.

As with any race, we can stumble or be sidetracked. In our race toward Christ we stumble over sin, a result of our fallen nature. In this unit we will see that sin is a part of all our lives, but not a part that has to destroy us.

We must first recognize sin and its effects in order to deal with it properly. Then we must learn the best ways to avoid sin and strengthen our virtues. We will also see that many others have gone before us and finished the great race.

THE STARTING LINE

Have you ever had a friend turn against you? Have you ever given someone a gift for which you were never thanked? How do you feel when these things happen? It's as though someone has told us we don't matter, that we're not important to him and he would just as soon forget us. It creates a division in our relationship. This is how we treat God when we sin. We turn on Him and are ungrateful for the many gifts He has given us.

Sin is disobeying and abusing His gifts. It's our personal choice to disconnect ourselves from the One who loves us the most. Would you purposely cut the wires on your headset when you were listening to a song you really liked? Not if you wanted to hear the music.

Do you ever purposely offend your best human friends? Of course not! You try always to please them. You want to make them happy. If Jesus is a friend, then every day you will try not to offend Him, but to please Him.

The Problem

Because we were given a free will and the ability to reason, we can make choices. This freedom gives us the ability to love and serve God. Freedom comes from putting our mind and will in charge of our emotions and passions. If we become slaves of our passions, we will not be free to choose wisely. For example, if Jason has an uncontrollable passion for video games, he will not choose board games or conversation time that may be good for him. By following a single-minded passion for video games, he has limited the number of free choices he can make about what to do with his free time, and he may hinder his ability to learn communication skills.

The part of our mind that tells us what is correct in a given situation is our conscience. Our conscience should be properly formed so we can take it with us wherever we go. Our conscience should not be confused with our feelings. Feelings indicate only pleasure

or pain, not right or wrong. Suppose I go into a grocery store. I know it is wrong to steal, but I feel hungry. What do I do? When I choose to follow my conscience and do what is right, I act correctly. When I do what my hunger tells me to do and act against what I know I should do, I sin. Sin is an offense against God. It is acting against my conscience.

Sin can further cloud our judgment and keep us from freely experiencing God's love.

Which of the following actions *really* makes you free? Underline your choices and explain why you made that choice.

1. Leaving home in anger **or** obeying your parents' rules _____

   _____

   _____

2. Lying to stay out of trouble **or** telling the truth and taking the consequences _____

   _____

   _____

3. Cheating to keep your grades up **or** doing your own work _____

   _____

   _____

4. Eating enough and enjoying it **or** eating more after you are already stuffed because you like the taste _____

   _____

   _____

5. Using drugs or alcohol to escape problems **or** facing problems and trying to solve them

   _____

   _____

   _____

The Law and Love

Rules are meant to protect us from making harmful mistakes we would regret later. God wrote His own Law on our hearts to protect us from giving in to temptation and doing wrong. The Ten Commandments spell out God's rules, which all people can recognize as good. Christ revealed the law's true meaning by showing us that love of God and neighbor is the reason for following the commandments.

God gave us the ability in our conscience to tell right from wrong, but our consciences must be formed in accordance with His Law of Love. Through Christ, we understand that love is the reason.

Read the Ten Commandments (Exodus 20:1-17).

1. Explain how the first three involve loving God.

   _____

   _____

   _____

   _____

   _____

   _____

   _____

   _____

2. Explain how the rest involve loving your neighbor._____

   _____

   _____

   _____

   _____

   _____

   _____

   _____

Compose a brief prayer to God, asking forgiveness for the times you failed to listen to your conscience, and thanking Him for giving us directions in the Ten Commandments.

_____

_____

_____

_____

_____

_____

_____

_____

The Solution

Sometimes our desires are so strong that it is difficult to choose what is right, but God always rewards us for our goodness. We must always work to form proper habits so we can resist temptation to sin. For example, if we always tell our parents the truth, then this habit will make it easier to overcome a temptation to lie

Maturity = Responsibility

to them. The stronger and more mature we become, the more we are able to make the proper decisions and the freer we become. This maturity comes from strengthening our relationship with Christ. He gives us the strength we need to avoid sin and act in ways pleasing to Him. A sign of maturity is our willingness to take responsibility for our own actions. When a mature person sins, he admits it and accepts the consequences. He doesn't make mistakes worse by lying to cover them up. Also, he learns from his mistakes. If he is caught sinning, he is grateful. The mature person thanks God that he was clearly shown his sin and then resolves never to do it again.

> To help you mature
> You have to work at being pure.
> Chastity is a virtue given to you
> To help you see the moral view.
> With this virtue you must use control
> No matter what is your moral goal.
> You have to work at chastity night and day
> and the only way you can do this is to pray
> Because God is good and God is great and
> You are the one who determines your fate.
>
> —Anna, age 17

Life: The Olympic Race

The importance of developing good habits in our spiritual life can be seen more clearly if we make the comparison between life and an Olympic race. Imagine yourself as a runner in training.

Runners take good care of their bodies by eating the right foods and running daily. When they're tempted to eat something harmful, they remember their goal and the need to have a healthy body. They learn to go on even when it hurts. They overcome the temptations to stop or give up. They know that if they want to "go for the gold", they must keep strengthening their muscles so they are ready for the "big race".

So too, in our race toward Heaven, we must have the proper "nourishment" and exercise our "muscles" of virtue daily. Our nourishment is the grace that comes from prayer and the sacraments, especially the Holy Eucharist. Strength will come from exercising the muscles of our soul through developing the virtues like temperance, chastity and honesty. Each time we overcome temptation our souls become stronger, and these virtues become more a part of us. We will be able to run for Jesus and win. We will gain much more than just gold.

chapter Thirteen

HURDLES ON THE TRACK TO HOLINESS

Temptation is not a sin. Temptation is an invitation to sin. Temptation comes when we're presented with a choice between God's will and something or someone else. Resisting temptation is a means of becoming a stronger person. Giving into temptation makes you feel guilty and sad. Resisting temptation helps you to feel better about yourself because you realize that you and God are in control. Every time you resist temptation, you become a stronger, freer person because you are winning a battle over sin. You are developing good habits, or human virtues, that are necessary for living a happy life.

Jesus was tempted by Satan, (see Hebrews 4:15). In the journey of earthly life, everyone in the human race will be tempted by Satan, the world and sometimes our own flesh. Feeling a temptation is different than falling for a temptation. Christ's

Where do you draw the line? If you put a frog in a bucket of hot water, it will jump out immediately. But if you put the frog in a bucket of cool water and heat the water up slowly, it will get *cooked!* The frog cannot judge at which precise point the water becomes *too hot*. Like a frog, many are never able to decide at what point to quit.

example shows us that we are able to jump these hurdles that are placed on the track to holiness. Many saints have faced great temptations and have resisted them. We can avoid the fall because we can decide to follow God with our free will. This involves sacrifice on our parts. The little sacrifices we make to resist temptation now can make us stronger people. Resisting temptation is a daily cross that we unite with Christ's Cross in order to prove our love for Him. Never forget that He gives us the grace to overcome temptation if only we ask. So decide: Whose side are you on? Choose Christ!

Life on earth offers a continuous battle between good and evil. Even in times when evil is popular, remember it is only the devil in disguise. You have to decide: Who is worth fighting for? Satan made his choice between God and himself and chose himself.

> No temptation has overtaken you that is not common to man. God is faithful, and he will not let you be tempted beyond your strength, but with the temptation will also provide the way of escape, that you may be able to endure it.
>
> —1 Corinthians 10:13

The good angels, the prophets, the Apostles and the saints chose God. One of the devil's favorite tactics is to try to confuse us as he did Adam and Eve. He might twist and turn things so that we might be deceived into thinking that something evil is really good, OK, or not that big of a deal. Don't be deceived! God wants you to choose Him because He made you to be happy with Him for all eternity.

One of the problems we inherited with the original sin is that we sometimes actually like to sin. Sin sometimes seems attractive or pleasurable. Depending on the personality or temperament we received, there are some sins that seem easier for us to commit than other sins. Some people enjoy being

> Be sober, be watchful. Your adversary the devil prowls around like a roaring lion, seeking some one to devour. Resist him, firm in your faith, knowing that the same experience of suffering is required of your brotherhood throughout the world.
>
> —1 Peter 5:8–9

lazy; some who might never be lazy might like to "put down" others to make themselves feel superior.

Pride, which is love of self more than God, is considered the core of all sins and is one of the seven capital sins. The seven capital sins are the roots of most of the other sins. They are: pride, lust, greed, envy, anger, sloth (laziness), gluttony (excessive eating). Think of the capital sins as weeds. We should try to pull out our sins at the root. If we know our tendencies to sin, we can work against those tendencies by developing an opposite virtue until the temptation is hardly there anymore.

Resisting temptation also includes thinking ahead and avoiding situations that may cause sin. We cannot presume that we are strong enough to resist the temptations of each day. If we do not want to sin, then we must avoid tempting situations. We can't romp through a field of poison ivy and then pray that we don't get a rash. If we put a hand over a fire, the question is not if we will get burned, it's *when*. The simplest solution is to stay away from the fire. If we develop the habit of dressing modestly, keeping our thoughts on worthwhile things and staying busy, the chances are good that we will stay pure and earn the true respect of our friends and peers.

Prayer and the sacraments are important weapons against sin in this war between good and evil. God wants to give us the strength to resist temptation. We just need to stay close to Him. Frequent prayer keeps us close to God. Without God's grace we are left only to human strength, and we can be defeated more easily. The Rosary is a pow-

erful prayer against sin and temptations of impurity. Frequent confession and Communion provide the grace to be stronger. Always turn to God with confidence and allow Him to help you resist temptations.

Finally, we should not be a source of temptation for others. We can sin by leading others into sin. Our responsibility is to lead others to Christ, not lead them into temptation. We must guard our purity and the purity of others with love of God and love of each other.

Read Ephesians 6:10–20 and answer the following questions.

1. Who and what does Saint Paul say we are fighting against? _____

   _____

   _____

   _____

   _____

2. What will help us win the fight? _____

   _____

   _____

   _____

   _____

   _____

3. What comprises the "armor of God"? _____

   _____

   _____

   _____

   _____

   _____

   _____

Resist Temptation Exercises

Can you help these teenagers make the right choices? Write what they should do to resist the temptations.

1. Mark is home alone after school. He turns on an afternoon TV show, but soon realizes that it is obscene. He can continue to watch the show since no one will know, or he can _____

    _____

    _____

2. Sue, who has a great figure, is invited to a co-ed beach party. She can wear the two-piece bikini she usually wears to sunbathe, or she can

    _____

    _____

3. Laura is baby-sitting with her new friend Cheryl at a home that has a VCR/DVD library of R-rated films. Cheryl asks Laura to select one to watch. Laura can choose an R-rated movie, or she can _____

    _____

    _____

4. Rob accepted an invitation to Jim's party. Later on in the week he hears that Jim's parents will not be home and that there will be girls and beer at the party. Rob can still go, or he can

    _____

    _____

    _____

5. Jennifer has a massive crush on Bill. Bill seems interested only in the basketball team and his science project. Jennifer can keep flirting with him until he is finally distracted, or she can

    _____

    _____

    _____

6. Mike has been given permission to go to Sylvia's house to study if one of her parents is home. When he gets to Sylvia's, Mike realizes both of her parents are gone. He can stay and study, or he can _____

    _____

    _____

Never give the devil a ride. . . He'll always want to drive.

Sexual temptation is nothing new to mankind. The Book of Proverbs in the Bible is an ancient collection of practical advice for wise living that includes warnings against hanging around with people who will lead us into temptation.

Look up these Proverbs verses, read them and write what you think is the strongest line from each one:

Proverbs 5:1–8 _____

_____

_____

Proverbs 6:20–29 _____

_____

_____

Proverbs 7 _____

_____

_____

Then write the answers to these questions:

1. What are these proverbs telling us to do? _____

_____

_____

2. What clues do the Proverbs give us about the way women try to lead men into temptation? _____

_____

_____

3. What are some ways men lead women into temptation?_____

_____

_____

4. What are some consequences of giving in to sexual temptation? _____

_____

_____

5. Write a proverb similar to these, but address it as a warning to "My daughter" instead of "My son".

_____

_____

_____

_____

_____

MODESTY: A GOOD "PUT-ON"

What do you put on to take a cake out of the oven? An oven mitt. What do you put on in the winter to go sledding? A heavy jacket. What do you put on to strengthen a weak ankle? An elastic bandage.

Modesty is like a good "put-on". You put on modesty to guard the senses so you can protect your purity and the purity of others. Purity is similar to chastity. Purity is focusing your attention on the love of God, avoiding the distractions of the world. Jesus said in the sixth Beatitude, "Blessed are the pure in heart, for they shall see God" (Matthew 5:8). Chastity and purity let us love God with an undivided heart. These virtues help us keep our love from becoming selfish.

In order for your body and soul to proclaim this virtue of chastity, you've got to prove it by your behavior! Prove to God that you can live up to His plan by practicing modesty.

For a Pure Mind: Stay Away from the Mind's Junk Food

The mind is an amazing gift. It has the ability to store information in the memory for us to use later. Caution: such information is not easily erased. What goes in is what comes out. That's a very simple principle of storage.

- If you fill your school locker with books and supplies, do you go there when you need your bicycle?
- If you fill your drawers with clothing and personal items, do you look there for your pet parakeet?
- If you fill your mind with images of passion, violence, rebellion and disobedience, can you go there for tenderness, concern, forgiving thoughts and faithfulness?

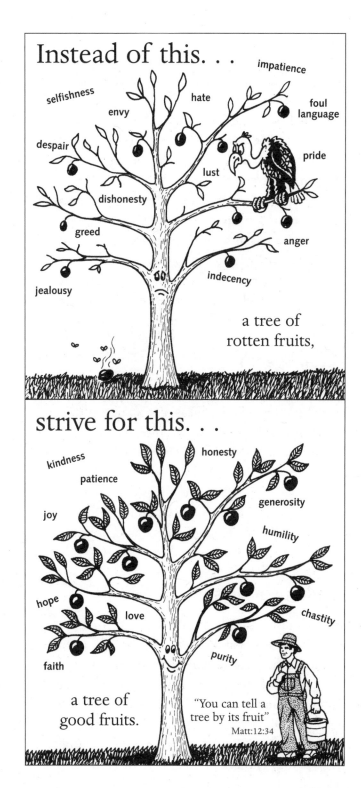

Instead of this. . . a tree of rotten fruits,

impatience
selfishness
hate
envy
foul language
despair
pride
lust
dishonesty
greed
anger
indecency
jealousy

strive for this. . . a tree of good fruits.

kindness
honesty
patience
joy
generosity
humility
hope
love
chastity
faith
purity

"You can tell a tree by its fruit"
Matt:12:34

> Blessed are the pure in heart,
> for they shall see God.
>
> —Matthew 5:8

Jesus says we can judge a tree by its fruit: "For out of the abundance of the heart the mouth speaks. The good man out of his good treasure brings forth good, and the evil man out of his evil treasure brings forth evil" (Matthew 12:34–35).

When we let in enough junk, the abnormal begins to seem normal. We even begin to believe that sin is normal, acceptable behavior, and then we have improperly formed our conscience. Immodesty and impurity stir up unhealthy curiosity in our mind that can lead us into more temptation than we would normally have had to overcome.

Modesty begins as an attitude of respect for love and life, and can also help the attitudes and behaviors of others to be pure.

Clean Speech

If we use "dirty" words when we talk about love and sexuality, how will our ideas of sexuality automatically become holy on our wedding day?

If we sound as if we're immature, how can we expect to be treated like mature people?

If we listen to talk and songs that are cheap and unChristian and that violate God's love, how are we going to learn the tender words that express His love to the one we love?

Modesty in Dress

By dressing modestly, we show people that we respect ourselves and others. We can let our true beauty shine from within. Modesty is in line with the dignity of the human person. We are made in the image and likeness of God, and are to dress and act accordingly as sons and daughters of the King of the Universe. Your God-given dignity should inspire your choices of what type of clothing to buy or wear. Think of what you are saying with the clothes you choose.

Immodest dress, including clothes that are tight, skimpy or transparent, can be a real temptation to others. Teenage girls often don't realize how quickly a boy's feelings and desires can be aroused. Men are turned on by their senses more easily than women are. Usually girls even act more flirty when they wear sexy clothes. Immodestly dressed girls could become an occasion of sin instead of the mirror of God's love and beauty that they should be.

Modesty certainly requires that we keep all of our clothes all the way on all of the time. This means zipped, buttoned, fastened and snapped. In dressing modestly, make sure that any private parts of your

> Put on Modesty: a pure mind, clean speech, modest dress, virtuous action.

Here's one that will make the guys drool... the "saran-wrap mini-bikini" only $95!

No thank you, I'm a young woman, *not* a cheese sandwich.

We're going to a bowling alley, not a swimsuit competition.

Look near the back of your Bible to find 1 Peter 3:3–4, and record what God sees as the hidden beauty of the heart in those who are reverent and chaste:

_____

_____

_____

_____

The ninth commandment teaches us about purity and modesty. Remember the ninth commandment? You shall not covet your neighbor's wife? And then Jesus even added more about purity when he said, "But I say to you that every one who looks at a woman lustfully has already committed adultery with her in his heart" (Matthew 5:28). Modesty is important because of our struggle between the desires of the body and the spirit. Young people who keep their heart purely focused on God will have a better chance of resisting temptation. This does not mean that those who date them can dress or act immodestly. One must help the other. Purity of intention means that we act in a way that shows we are seeking God's will for us and those around us.

Whether it is provoked by an ad on a shopping bag or in a magazine, by slang words used in TV shows or movies, or by a sign for a dance club that

body cannot be seen. Clothe yourselves with dignity. Modesty can mean being dressed in pure style.

We can wear stylish clothes that are not immodest. We can watch out not to wear tight clothes, exposed navels or T-shirts with words on them that suggest sexual immorality. Guys and gals should also be careful that the ways they walk, stand, dance or carry themselves are not viewed by others as an invitation to lustful thoughts.

Immodest dress can stir up unhealthy curiosities that lead to lust. Lust is a desire to sexually use people instead of loving them. If we dress, talk or act immodestly, and advertise the wrong meaning of our sexuality, we lose the freedom of knowing if others like us simply for who we are. Do you want to be considered a "sexy thing", or do you want to be known as a good person? Isn't it much better to get people's attention with our goodness than to "lure" them improperly with our looks or clothes? How do you want people to think of you?

None of us would go out and deliberately hurt one of our close friends. But don't we do this every time we tell a dirty joke? We make fun of our and their sexuality, and little by little we start thinking of sex as a joke. Soon we are so calloused to these kinds of things that our set of morals changes and we begin to spread this around to others and cheapen their lives.

Our sexuality is not a joke. It is a gift from God and one to be used wisely. If you were given a paintbrush, wouldn't it be better to use it constructively to paint a picture, than destructively to paint graffiti on a wall? The same is true about our sexuality. We can use it constructively by respecting our sexuality as well as the sexuality of others.

Always talk and think about these matters with care and reverence because they are gifts from God.

—Betsy, age 16

Give us clean hearts and minds, O Lord, so we can look each other in the eye. . .

Custody of the eyes (or purity of vision, as it is called in the *Catechism*) is a way of disciplining one's feelings and imagination when tempted with impure thoughts. Anyone can practice this by looking away from sexy advertisements, turning off sexually suggestive music, and using quick game reflexes on the TV remote control when an immodest scene appears on the screen. If immodest scenes come into the mind that may have been seen in the past, you can "change the channel" in your brain instead of letting your imagination take off with the scene and the feelings it can bring. A little prayer at this time will help a lot.

We live in a culture that makes money from exploiting the human body. It exposes to everyone those intimate scenes that should rightly remain private and personal. Modesty protects the mystery and privacy of the human person and of personal love relationships. Modesty requires a certain amount of privacy for ourselves that keeps us from becoming too familiar with our date. Deeper levels of personal intimacy should be reserved for marriage.

Christians who practice modesty of speech, eyes and clothing inspire a way of life that resists the allurements of a world that misunderstands the truth and meaning of human sexuality.

You may be wondering how you fit into this chastity picture if you are not yet old enough to date. Maybe you don't think this has much to do with you today. But whether you're in middle school or in high school, what you decide today and the habits you begin forming will affect you throughout your life. This is the same body and mind you will

exploits people's bodies, teens may be exposed to many ideas that are disrespectful of the human person. How do we sort these out and resist the temptations that are around us?

You may hear one of those lies of the devil that says, "Oh, I'm only 'looking', not doing anything wrong." Why is this form of immodesty still wrong? Because lustful looks are rooted in the way we see others—as tools for our pleasure, instead of children of God. Using others for pleasure is not in accordance with human love and dignity, whether it's with the eyes, imagination or in person. What is harbored in the mind will later come out in behavior.

take to your future vocation of celibacy or marriage. This is the same soul you will have for all eternity. Keep it pure. Focus purely on Christ's love instead of the world's misinterpretation of love.

One of the purposes of this book is to challenge you to think about God's love for you and His plan for His love in your life. Because He loves us, He wants us to **choose chastity**.

Whether or not you've started dating, you can choose a chaste manner of life now by:

- Choosing TV shows, movies, records, magazines and books that are good and pure
- Avoiding the media influences that make immorality look and sound glamorous
- Keeping your speech clean
- Dressing modestly
- Behaving as Jesus, Mary and the saints would act
- Realizing that God loves you and has a plan for your life
- Asking God's help to resist temptations and to have the grace to follow Him
- Learning to love God more and more each day
- Trusting God that He will fulfill the deepest longings of your heart and guide you to the vocation that is right for you
- Avoid leading others into temptation

Let's activate the truth!
Put good thoughts into words

1. Write an essay or discuss ways that you can apply the following Scripture verses to your life today:

   Proverbs 4:23–27
   Keep your heart with all vigilance;
      for from it flow the springs of life.
   Put away from you crooked speech,
      and put devious talk far from you.
   Let your eyes look directly forward,
      and your gaze be straight before you.
   Take heed to the path of your feet,
      then all your ways will be sure.
   Do not swerve to the right or to the left;
      turn your foot away from evil.

   Proverbs 13:3
   He who guards his mouth preserves his life;
      he who opens wide his lips comes to ruin.

2. Write a short poem about purity or modesty.

3. Make a list of five things that you or your friends can do now to combat immodesty and impurity in our culture. (One idea was carried out by a group of high school girls in Arizona. The girls collected signatures on a petition to the management of a large department store asking them to buy more modest clothes that were also in style. The store responded and discovered a designer who would take the current fashions and colors and add more material.)

4. Make a list of five things that guys or gals can do with a career in the future that could help combat the impurity of our culture.

5. Write out the three sentences from numbers 2531 and 2533 in the *Catechism*. Write three more sentences in your own words on what modesty does for us; what it requires, and what it protects.

chapter Fifteen

THE CHASTITY GENERATION

Growing numbers of teens today are choosing to practice chastity. In spite of a sex-saturated culture, young people are seeing the benefits of loving others in a pure and chaste way. Especially after seeing friends and relatives suffer from choosing the superficial ways of the sinful world, young people find that the beauty of chastity can be even more appealing. Those who love Christ are attracted to the light.

Dare to be different! While practicing chastity, your dating years will be countercultural, which means against the culture. The culture sets out self-centered dating "rules" that are blasted through movies, magazines and music. They announce "How to get someone", and they presume dating means stirring up sexual desires by dressing or acting immodestly. For the Christian, dating is a time to develop friendships with people who will help lead you *toward* God, not away from Him. Otherwise, dating would be a waste of time, a series of heartbreaks, or a temptation to sin.

Most teens prefer chaperoned games, dances and parties as ways to get together instead of going on single dates. Other teens, busy with studies, sports and other activities, don't have time for nights out, but still socialize with friends. Many young Christians are choosing not to date at all until they are closer to the age when they want to marry, in order to avoid distractions to their educational goals or to keep from unnecessary heartaches. All of this is normal.

Our social life as teens helps us learn more about other people and introduces us to other families. We can develop insight and greater understanding of people as we learn about another person's background and interests.

Socializing with others also gives us an opportunity to practice respect for the opposite sex. It helps us learn about ourselves as we compare our likes

Okay, so when you're chaste, does that mean you can't even date?

No, Sean, dating can be good! You can develop virtues while you're dating.

and dislikes, values and future hopes with those of other people. We can practice being with the opposite sex as a friend, not just an object of affection, when we focus on learning the communication skills we will need for a lifetime.

Well-planned and thoughtful dating can be a training ground for chastity. It is not necessary to lock yourself in a closet to keep your love pure. It *is* necessary to develop self-mastery in new ways that we didn't need to practice as a child. It is necessary to pray for the grace to stay pure and good. People who choose to date can still help train one another in the character trait of self-control by not placing themselves in compromising situations that could lead to temptation and sin. This positive training can last for a lifetime, so that after marriage when the going gets tough, we are strong enough to practice self-control in other new areas of life.

These years should be fun! At this age social gatherings, group dates or even double dates are preferable to one-on-one dating. This is no time to get serious, when marriage is still a long way off.

How Do You Know If You Are Ready to Date?

Here's a handy checklist:

- Do your parents think you practice emotional maturity?
- Are you good at self-discipline?
- Are you kind and patient with your family and friends?
- Do you have good conversation skills?
- Do you have a number of friendships with teens of your own sex and with the opposite sex?
- Have you reached the dating age according to your family rules? (This often means being old enough to drive and having a job to earn money to pay for the date!)
- Are you responsible and obedient at home and at school?
- Do you know and practice high moral standards?
- Are you honest with your parents?
- Have you proven to your parents that you can make good decisions on your own?
- Can you stick to your religious values even under pressure not to?
- Do you know enough people with solid moral values that would be worth your time to date?
- Do you have the time to spare from your family, school and personal activities?
- Can you afford it financially?

- Can you go out and have fun without doing anything immoral or illegal?
- Have you discussed curfew and dating rules with your parents, and are you clear about the consequences for disobeying the rules?

These are some of the things you and your parents should consider when deciding if you are mature enough to date.

Many other chapters in this book have helped provide you with information to grow in maturity, so that your dating years will be happy. Knowing yourself, as discussed in Chapter 7, will help you see what strengths or weaknesses you bring to a relationship, what you need to work on before you date, and what to avoid in a date that would bring out the worst in you. The standards of friendship from Chapter 9 would also be a good review before dating. The purpose of dating in the teen years is to develop friendships with the opposite sex, not to steal sexual pleasures from someone who is not your spouse. Knowing the standards of love (Chapter 8) and the different communication skills of the opposite sex (Chapter 6) would also be good to know and review as the years go on. More importantly, you should have your emotional life in order, as outlined in Chapter 10. Most important would be to know and believe that God's plan is far different from, but better than, the world's plan for dating. Without emotional maturity and sexual morality, dating would be a destructive instead of constructive activity for someone of any age.

Single dating gets to be serious business, because it involves our emotions. It's more than just fun and games. People's hearts get involved. When people date before they are ready they risk:

- Mistaking emotional feelings for love
- Feeling trapped and not having the courage to break up
- Neglecting good friends, whom they need
- Feeling controlled by another person
- Getting possessive of another person
- Leaving family in the background
- Being hurt or hurting another
- Liking someone more than one is liked
- Looking on every member of the opposite sex only as a potential romance, and that way missing out on some good friendships

It's smart to wait for single dating until the early adult years when we have more maturity to help us deal with the emotions and pressures involved. Teens today have enough pressures without the addition of an emotional relationship. For now, it's good to enjoy working on your own character, being with friends, and focusing on your education.

Romantic attractions will come and go in life. It is not necessary to be anxious about them or hang on to them, thinking that no one else will ever come along. Trust God and stay very close to Him so that He will guide you. Fewer than 10 percent of people marry their high school sweetheart, and even 40 percent of engagements are broken. Yet people do survive and later find the love that God has prepared for them.

Before falling head over heels into a romantic attachment, keep in your head the knowledge that feelings of infatuation are not really love. With time and maturity, however, they could possibly lead there. Infatuation can be fun, but don't confuse it with real love.

INFATUATION	LOVE
Being "in love with love"	Growing in a relationship based on interests and values you share
Self-centered	Selfless and self-giving
Based in feelings	Caring for the good of the other person more than your own wishes
Immature: "I can't live without you." Possessive or jealous	Mature: Grows stronger through trials and resisting temptations
One-sided or short-lived	Mutual giving that increases with time
Having a crush on someone	Best described in the Bible in 1 Corinthians (chapter 13) as patient, kind, not jealous, not a show-off, not rude

Virtue in Action

Most important, if you choose to date, go out only with people who openly practice chastity and let them know you practice chastity, too. If you are always disagreeing on your guidelines of affection, you will not learn about real love. Most likely, the person putting on the pressure will eventually wear you down to join in sin. Sin is the opposite of love. Real love is not

> Love is patient. Waiting for marriage can be a joy for those who really love.

possible in sexual activity outside the Sacrament of Matrimony because premarital sex is outside the laws of God, Who is Love. Don't kid yourself!

Practice the virtue of chastity. With your self-control and God's help, this virtue is possible and livable. Virtues are good habits that make "doing the right thing" easier. Virtues help us keep our passions under control and help us exercise self-control.

Saying yes to love means saying no to premarital sex.

Self-Control

The world's view of dating selfishly "to get someone" is not in God's plan. It's just not right. Paul wrote to the Galatians:

> Now the works of the flesh are plain: immorality, impurity, licentiousness, idolatry, sorcery, enmity, strife, jealousy, anger, selfishness, dissension, party spirit, envy, drunkenness, carousing, and the like. . . . But the fruit of the Spirit is love, joy, peace, patience, kindness, goodness, faithfulness, gentleness, self-control. (Galatians 5:19–23a)

Think of the people you know who are dating. Are they examples of self-indulgence, or do they live the fruits of the Holy Spirit? Which one of these is really love?

If you don't know anyone who wants to respect you, it's better not to date at all. We can't tempt ourselves with unchaste dating partners and impure pleas-ures and just hope we stop at the right time. We have a free will to choose what is good. We know what situations lead us in the wrong direction. So we can choose to set up the right ones. "Resist the devil and he will flee from you" (James 4:7).

So, when you are looking for dating advice, should you go to the latest teenage movie, read the hottest magazine or listen to the sexiest song? Not if you want what is best for you! Let's look at some positive dating guidelines that can help us learn more about communication and relationships. Setting standards before you date is the best way to practice chastity while dating.

Dating Do's and Don'ts for the Chastity Generation

Discuss these points with your parents and see if they have any to add.

1. **Do be selective about when and whom you date.** It is not good to "fall" for everyone who gives us attention. It is better to set standards of character for people you might date—and don't lower your standards because you are lonely or want affection. Get to know people at a level of friendship so that you know them well before you let feelings of romance get stirred up.

2. **Do practice eye contact.** Eye contact helps you see another other person through the eyes of his soul. People who cannot maintain eye contact may have troubles with personal intimacy, self-knowledge or honesty. Ask yourself if this person is mature enough for a real dating friendship. Couples who skip the eye contact at the beginning of a relationship will have bigger troubles later.

3. **Do learn and practice good verbal communication.** Communication skills are more than a language arts section on the Standardized Achievement Test! Communication is about expressing your thoughts and ideas, bouncing them off another person's brain in order to hear

that person's thoughts and ideas. Good Christian relationships do not include gossip or talk about other people. Beginning relationships stay at the level of "small talk" about things, or likes and dislikes of music and clothes. Growing friendships involve discussing ideas and plans that make us better people or improve society. A friend also listens carefully to the other.

Words should be **kind and affirming,** or expressing understanding and patience. They should not be sarcastic, put downs or criticisms.

Express yourself verbally, not physically. This could be your key to success throughout life. It's good to develop the ability to express yourself now. Teens who spend more time kissing or watching movies than they do talking are heading down the wrong road for good dating.

4. **Express affection without passion.** Hugging someone you care about is still part of friendly affection, but embracing that person passionately can stir up arousing feelings. Keep kisses short and hands in view. Prolonged kissing or anything that purposefully causes sexual arousal is sinful outside of marriage. It just makes people want more; so avoid leading yourselves into temptation. You can keep cool on a date if you want to. If you're struggling with temptation, then end

the date and go home. (It's better to go in, than sin!) Remind yourself that you are with a person who has a 90 percent chance of becoming someone else's husband or wife. Imagine a video of your dates with that person given as a wedding present. How do you wish someone would treat your future husband or wife? God's plan is that we arrive at our vocation in purity.

5. **Do be prudent about where you go.** Certainly, modesty and chastity require that we never entertain friends of the opposite sex in a house where parents are not home, in a bedroom, or in a horizontal position—yes, even while watching a movie. This precaution protects us from leading ourselves or others into temptation. If you're too tired to sit up for a whole date, then you're too tired to date; so go home.

6. **Do learn to work together.** Teamwork on school projects, youth group work and family chores are important elements in friendships and relationships. Working together is one of the things that help you find out if this person is worth spending more time with. Can the two of you work together to accomplish some good? It might be a yearbook page or service project or science fair display for now, but it's an indication of the type of people with whom you work well.

The skills of eye contact, verbal communication with kindness and goodness, and teamwork will end up becoming much more important during the dating years than those items in the secular magazines or TV shows on the worldly view of dating.

7. **Do be virtuous—which means good!** Do you think that "sexiness" will attract a person who will love you like Christ? Or will your virtue attract a person who knows real love? Think about it. Your goodness and virtue, cheerfulness and kindness will ultimately draw others to you much more than the right lipstick, mouthwash, clothes or set of muscles. Your kindness, patience, honesty, responsibility and trustworthi-

ness will help you attract people who have those qualities, too.

8. **Honor God and your father and mother while dating.** What does God and the fourth commandment have to do with this? The commandment did not come with an amendment saying "only when they're looking" or "only when you're young". Ask yourself, "Would my parents approve if they saw me now?" And, because He is always with us, we ask, "Is God pleased with me now?"

9. **Plan your dates well.** Don't leave the house without scheduled plans. Practice double dating or group dating to add to the fun and avoid private temptations. Discuss plans with your date ahead of time, and tell your parents where you will be. Think ahead to avoid private times that may present temptation. Only do things that help you become a better person. Ask your parents what time they want you home, and follow their curfew rules. Your date will appreciate it, too.

10. **Make a firm decision now to practice chastity,** and date only people who believe the same way. You will give the gift of your virginity only once, so follow God's plan and do so only in marriage. Your dating years will be much happier and freer. Carry yourself with dignity. Be an example of real love. Join the chastity generation!

More Dating Tips for the Chastity Generation

1. **Don't kiss everyone you date.** Kisses are for solid relationships, not just for fun or saying good night. Besides, they stir up additional emotions of attraction. To some people today, a kiss is no more meaningful than a baton exchange on a track relay. They'll kiss anyone who is around. Don't give away affection without sincerity and meaning. Remember that you are special; the Lord dwells in you. You're too good to be cheap. Kissing is not a game. You

> On the night of my wedding,
> I want to be able to say to my beloved,
> "I loved you …before I knew you…
> enough to save myself for you.
> I give myself only to you.
> No one has ever gone this way before.
> My love for you, my gift for you,
> is pure and true."

are a temple of the Holy Spirit, not a target for predators or a toy for fun.

2. **Don't get so serious!** In the type of group dating that usually takes place in the early teen years, guys and gals should not have to worry about making "moves." Slow down! The only thing you need to "prove" to your date is your purity and goodness. Try not to own, smother or control the time or emotions of the person you like. The teen years are a time to have fun with friends, not to feed our insecurities or get emotionally distracted. Let your dates be free to like you and others. Keep yourself free to be yourself, know yourself and improve yourself.

3. **Don't arouse your date's passions.** Almost every embrace on TV includes a passionate, mouth-mangling scene. That is not romance! That is not affection! Affection includes the same kind of greeting that you might give a long-lost brother or sister. You're happy to see him, but not trying to turn him on. God invented passion for married couples, not dates. Be respectful of your partner's purity by avoiding arousal. The Song of Solomon in the Bible reminds us not to awaken love before its time. Sexual passions can bond a couple together, not only making a future break-up more devastating, but also confusing them about whether they are the right person for each other. Never offend someone's purity by

> Pray: Lord, be with me and help me. Fill me with your grace. Be there with me in times of temptation. Help me to avoid and resist all that is evil. Help me to truly reflect your love to the world. Amen.

stirring up that person's passions. Be patient and wait until marriage.

4. **Don't even think about anything indecent.**
   This is not just a suggestion anymore; this one is a direction for avoiding deliberate sexual sin. Never touch another person in a private part of that person's body, whether in or through the person's clothes, with your hand or mouth or anything. It is sinful outside of marriage to deliberately look at or touch a private part of someone's body or to allow another to see or touch yours. (A private part is one that is covered by a modest bathing suit.) Keep your private parts private. Keep the sacred embrace sacred by waiting until marriage. For the dating years, keep all of your clothes all the way on, all of the time—until your honeymoon. After the wedding, when you are husband and wife, it is the time for giving yourself totally to one another.

How Will This Make Me Happy?

Following the laws of God makes us happier people. This is difficult sometimes and may not be popular. People may make fun of us for following God's will instead of theirs. But we will like ourselves more in the long run whenever we obey God, because we were made for Him and pleasing Him is in our nature.

We have a free will to choose to practice purity. Every animal has instincts and desires. Only human beings are responsible for their own actions. Our minds and wills prevail over our biology, and when we control our strongest desires, then we are fulfilling our human potential. Self-control is also called self-mastery. Pope John Paul II taught that only when we

Sandy wrote:

Virginity is the ideal of wholeness and integrity. Giving your body to someone expresses total commitment. This union is only truthful and meaningful after you are sacramentally, legally, socially, emotionally and spiritually committed in marriage.

So the question is, do you want to give your whole self to your future husband or wife? Marriage is like giving a gift. Let's say you want to give your friend a radio for his birthday, but before you do, you decide to keep the speaker for yourself. So before wrapping it, you take off the cover and remove the speaker.

The next day your friend opens the gift and loves the looks of the radio but then finds there is something very important missing—the speaker. Your friend is cheated out of enjoying the total value of the gift.

If we abandon chastity and give up our virginity before marriage, we are cheating our future husbands/wives and not giving them our total selves. It's up to us to choose wholeness.

achieve self-mastery can we truly love. The *Catechism* puts it this way:

> The virtue of chastity comes under the cardinal virtue of *temperance*, which seeks to permeate the passions and appetites of the senses with reason. (*CCC* 2341)

Self-mastery is a long and exacting work. One can never consider it acquired once and for all. It presupposes renewed effort at all stages of life (see Titus 2:1–6). The effort required can be more intense in certain periods, such as when the personality is being formed during childhood and adolescence. (*CCC* 2342)

There it is from the *Catechism*—that self-mastery is part of our job as teenagers. This is where we Christians are going against the culture again. Much of the modern world thinks that teenage dating is a time to be out of control, and the Church asks us to use this as a time to learn self-control. You know the best choice. Will it be Christ or the world?

In your Bible, look up 1 Peter 2:11 and write it here.

_____

_____

_____

_____

_____

_____

Now underline the last five words. Then think about the decisions you have made this week and answer this question: "Were most of your decisions based on the needs of your **body** or the needs of your **soul**?"

PROJECTS

1. Use your imagination to advertise virtue. Think up a catchy phrase that promotes the virtue of chastity. Create a poster or banner to display in your classroom or at home on your bulletin board. Make sure your message is respectful.

2. Practice using positive eye contact in communication. Do this with one of your friends, a parent or brother or sister. Sit across the table and try expressing feelings or ideas with your eye contact instead of with words. Have the other person guess which feeling or idea you are trying to express. Notice how you look at each other in the eye when you are saying something honest and good. See how differently you look each other in the eye while you are lying. Learn about communication and people through their eyes.

NATURE NEVER FORGIVES

God's Laws Are Designed to Protect Us, Not to Restrict Us

Whenever we sin, we offend God, harm ourselves and hurt other people. We damage our relationships as well as our own natures. Because we disturb the natural order that God created, there are many natural consequences that directly affect us, particularly with regard to sins against chastity.

Positive Consequences of Chastity

First, let's just list a few of the natural benefits of chastity:

- Keeps us free and pure to be open to God's vocational call
- Gives us time to learn about real friendship and communication
- Develops self-control (the cardinal virtue of temperance)
- Improves chances of a successful marriage
- Increases confidence and trust in our friends and, once we are married, our spouses

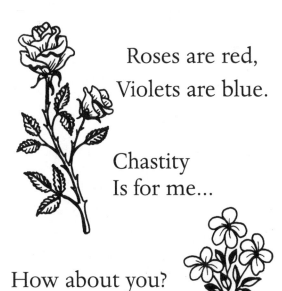

Roses are red,
Violets are blue.

Chastity
Is for me...

How about you?

- Promotes better unity within marriage
- Prevents infection from sexually transmitted diseases
- Eliminates worry
- Provides freedom to grow in maturity and integrity
- Gives key to moral, emotional and spiritual growth
- Keeps us from sin
- Gives the joy of obeying God

Negative Consequences of Sins against Chastity

The natural consequences of sins against chastity are evident all around us. The list looks overwhelming, but let's consider it anyway.

Emotional consequences

- Guilt, doubt, regret
- Depression, bitterness, distrust
- Disappointment in ourselves and others

- A sense of "clinging" to relationships rather than building relationships of mutual interests and concern
- A "broken heart"
- Memories that we can't erase
- Confusion about our relationships
- Difficulty learning about true love

Personal consequences

- Leads to insecurity or false sense of security
- Causes loss of self-control
- Puts us in the habit of "using" people
- Slows our personal, emotional, moral and spiritual growth
- Slows, and sometimes stops, our educations
- Stunts our ability to communicate at a mental level because we are using only our bodies

Social consequences

- Slows growth of the relationship
- Ruins reputations at a time when we need acceptance
- Breaks down our openness with our families
- Promotes dishonesty
- Reduces our interest in having fun with our friends
- May lead to an early marriage that is based on guilt or a pregnancy rather than on real love
- May fool us into marrying the wrong person

Physical consequences

- Sexually transmitted diseases, which are widespread today
- Infertility; possibility of developing problems conceiving children later in life
- Pregnancy, when we are not ready for the profound responsibility of caring for a child
- Consumes the energy we need for studying, sports, work and play

Is this love?
Is this life?

Fighting Fire with Fire

Some people suggest that contraception is the cure for reducing the negative consequences of sins against chastity. However, we should consider the *whole* picture and the whole person. Pregnancy is not a sin; fornication is! Our goal is not just to avoid consequences, but to live with integrity and wholeness. Besides, contraception causes its own problems. In addition to the spiritual and emotional harm, it can cause temporary and sometimes permanent damage to a teen's growing body. Contraception is artificial birth control. The word *artificial* itself tells us that it is unnatural. It is true that not everything artificial is wrong, but contraception is against the laws of God, which means that it is sinful. No matter how you look at it, contraception is full of negative consequences.

Peace and Justice: Consequences of the Heart and Soul

Although there are noticeable physical consequences of sexual sins, the consequences to the heart that may go unnoticed are sometimes the most confusing and devastating. Persons who choose to act on their passions will become unhappy. The *Catechism* tells us: "Chastity includes an *apprenticeship in self-mastery* which is a training in human freedom. The alternative is clear: either man governs his passions and finds peace, or he lets himself become dominated by them and becomes unhappy" (*CCC* 2339; see Sirach 1:22). That is exactly the opposite of what the world is telling us about sexual passion! The truth is that happiness, peace and freedom are really found through chastity.

Just Rewards

Besides finding peace through a life of chastity, we will be practicing the cardinal virtue of justice. An easy term for justice is fairness. It is not fair to steal sexual pleasures from someone. Sexual pleasure is a gift from God to married couples who give their whole lives to each other and are open to the creation of new life. Fornication is a sin against both love and justice.

Let's compare this to the case of a just inheritance. Suppose you come from a very wealthy family, and when you turn eighteen, your parents are planning to give you a million dollars. Suppose you are now only sixteen, and you become impatient and don't want to wait for the million you think you deserve. So you find a way through your computer to access your parents' bank account and begin stealing the money. They don't notice right away, and you are happy to be able to buy everything that you want. You think everything is fine, and ignore your conscience, which says you have betrayed your parents. Then when you turn seventeen, you get caught. Your parents are deeply offended by your dishonesty and betrayal, and the bank presses felony charges. You are tried as an adult and sent to prison by the justice system. You get out on your eighteenth birthday, and although your parents love you and have forgiven you, they have canceled your million-dollar gift. It cost them so much to pay the lawyers for your trial, and then there were the costs of the phone calls and visits to prison. The additional toll on their health due to the stress of being betrayed by their child was costly. It also cost the government money to keep you in prison, not to mention the cost of your heart being hardened by the prison experience. Many people paid a price for your impatience and desire to have material pleasures right away. The scene of your eighteenth birthday is different than it could have been had you waited.

Stealing sexual pleasures outside of marriage is unjust. You don't *deserve* sexual pleasure; it is a *gift* from God. It is one that He says must stay within the time and place He designed, and He will bless you with His grace when you live according to His plan.

Suppose God's plan for you was to be a priest, and in your confusion you didn't hear His call. You settle for a vocation that doesn't make you as happy. Or, suppose your vocation was to marriage, but because of your confusion about love, you marry a person who is not right for you and end up with years of misery. To steal the pleasures of marriage when you are not married is to betray God and His beautiful plan for you. It is also a betrayal of your future spouse if marriage is your vocation later on.

The experience of the "prison" of sexual sin takes many forms: addictions to using people or using pornography; the addiction to sexual pleasure; difficulties in really knowing your true vocation when you cannot purely hear God's call; confusion about whether a relationship is the best one for you at this time. Sexual sin is a huge step backward on the road to maturity and holiness. It is a prison you can easily avoid. It's time to *thank* God for his commandments.

We **do** know how to avoid these negative consequences—through **chastity.**

> Chastity means the successful integration of sexuality within the person and thus the inner unity of man in his bodily and spiritual being. (*CCC* 2337)

Christ gave it to me!
Helps me to become mature
And protects me from any diseases.
Sexual self-control
The virtue by which I regulate my sexual acts
Invites me to become one with God and myself
Tries to guide me, not restrict me.
Yes, I choose chastity!

—Lori-Ann, 15

chapter Seventeen

CLOSE ENCOUNTERS OF THE BEST KIND

The strength to lead a pure life comes from our personal relationship with Jesus Christ. Beside our daily prayer life, there are two sacraments we can receive often that give us close encounters of the best kind.

"It's Not My Fault!"

Since guilt separates us from God, He has given us the Sacrament of Penance to remove guilt and help us avoid sinning again. Guilt is the result of knowing we have done something wrong. Although our first reaction to guilt often is to blame others, the mature way to handle guilt is to admit mistakes and correct them. Jesus, the Great Counselor, uses our guilt to push us into an honest examination of our faults and find comfort from Him.

The Sacrament of Penance

The Catholic Church offers a unique opportunity to experience God's mercy in the Sacrament of Penance. There are three steps to this sacrament.

1. **Contrition.** We must be sorry for our sins. This sorrow can be caused by either fear of punishment or love of God. (Love is, of course, the better reason.) True sorrow means that we want to make up for our sin and try never to do it again.

2. **Confession.** We must confess our sins to a priest. When we examine our consciences and confess our sins, we face ourselves and our faults. No sin is too small or too big to confess to God in this sacrament. The priest represents Christ and gives us Christ's own forgiveness and healing. It is the words of the priest, "…I absolve you from your sins…" (that is, your sins are forgiven), that come directly from Christ and are our greatest source of consolation. Without the priest we could not hear those words from Christ.

3. **Satisfaction.** We must follow through with the penance the priest gives. God has forgiven us; He has removed the guilt, and He has cleared the path for us to renew our bonds with Him and the others whom we may have hurt. Reconciliation helps us find real peace in our lives.

Develop the habit of regular confession. Many have found that the grace they receive through this sacrament gives them strength to live the life Christ wants them to live. Don't cheat yourself out of this marvelous gift of God.

Here's what Jim, a high school junior, wrote about the consequences of sin:

I think that a lot of Christians don't really appreciate what a good God we have. He gives us good directions. Why not follow them?

Many of you may be thinking, "I'll do whatever I feel like doing", even though what you feel like doing may not be best for you.

Maybe it'll help if you can understand this sentence: *God's laws are designed to protect us, not to restrict us.*

Just think about that with the "sex only in marriage" rules. God wants to protect us from things like herpes, VD, being hurt, feeling used or being a teenage parent.

Besides those consequences, we have to suffer the spiritual consequences, too. When you sin, you can sometimes feel yourself getting further away from God, until eventually you don't care at all. Breaking one of God's sexuality laws, or any of His laws, can bring about a "foggy connection" between you and God.

God is always trying to reach out to us, but in our sin, we are resisting His invitation. You may feel ashamed of yourself, and not good enough for God, but He wants your love. That's why He gives us a chance to confess.

The Sacrament of Penance is a great one—one we don't take advantage of enough. So if you can't hear God, you may have moved too far away. Have the courage to go to confession.

These are some examples of sins against chastity:

- Dressing immodestly
- Reading obscene literature
- Telling or listening to a dirty joke
- Opening clothes that reveal private parts
- Entertaining impure thoughts in your mind
- Viewing immoral TV, movies or websites
- Passionate kissing before marriage
- Touching someone to arouse him or her sexually
- Talking disrespectfully about sexuality

> Confession is agreeing with God, saying "You are right. I was wrong. I'm sorry. Please forgive me."

Nourishment for the Race

Another tremendous source of strength to resist temptation is to experience true intimacy with God in the Eucharist. Jesus really comes to each of us in Holy Communion. He listens to us, speaks to us and strengthens us to live God's plan for our lives. As we obey His command to receive His Body and Blood, we are united with Him in a true bond of love and life.

ACT OF CONTRITION
O my God, I am heartily sorry
for having offended Thee,
and I detest all my sins,
because of Thy just punishments,
but most of all,
because they offend Thee, my God,
Who art all good and deserving
of all my love.
I firmly resolve,
with the help of Thy grace,
to confess my sins,
to do penance
and to amend my life. Amen.

The Mass celebrates Christ's ultimate sacrifice of love for us. In turn, we actually unite ourselves with Jesus and offer ourselves to the Father. We don't have to dream about what it would have been like if we had lived at the time of Christ. **Now is the time of Christ!**

Attending Mass as often as possible is the best training for the Olympic race of life. The Eucharist is the greatest health food, so much better for us than the junk food of the mind. It helps us over the hurdles of temptation and strengthens the habits of virtue.

Our presence at Mass allows us to experience the community of love that Christ gives to us in our parish. Being involved in the Church can give us the support we need to practice goodness. At times when our purity is being challenged, we can receive encouragement from our fellow Christians.

God the Father really loves us far more than we realize. He wants to be close to us. He is always there waiting for us to love Him in return. God's love is bigger than our sin, than our loneliness and our confusion. He wants us to experience His real, true love and to share it with others.

For strength to grow in the virtue of chastity, receive Christ: through the grace of confession, through His presence in the Eucharist and through the support of His Church. These truly are close encounters of the best kind.

chapter Eighteen

THE SAINTS COME MARCHING IN

In choosing chastity you certainly won't be alone. There are many saints in heaven who have finished the great race, and many living saints on earth who are still on the right track.

Movies, TV and radio would like us to believe that everyone is sexually immoral. And certain groups of teens may think they have to "talk big" about sexuality in order to be popular. The truth is just the opposite! In fact, more and more people are choosing chastity every day. Some people discover its benefits from the beginning, others have learned from their mistakes.

Many young people today appreciate God's plan for chastity because they have already set their minds and hearts on Christ. They know that purity is God's plan for them, and they want to please God. Some have seen their older brothers and sisters suffer from sins of impurity and don't want to make the same mistakes. Still others are motivated by fear of pregnancy, diseases, heartbreak or damaged reputation. Whatever our motives are, practicing chastity is important to God, and today's saints are an example for us.

Saints Are Heroes for God

Saint Maria Goretti is one of the many virgins who was martyred. Her love for God was so deep that she never wanted to offend him. Maria was only twelve years old when she was martyred because she

We may not be asked to die for Christ like St. Maria Goretti, but we may need to stand up for our beliefs. **If the television and movies threaten our purity by cheapening sex, do we have the courage to turn off the TV or walk out of the theater?** This does not require the strength that the martyrs have shown, but it requires a certain amount of heroism. **All Christians are given the strength necessary to lead a pure life.**

Throughout history, people of the Church have been role models of pure love for God. There were many teenaged saints: St. Agnes, St. Tarcisius, St. Stanislaus and St. Dominic Savio all put the love of God before anything else in their lives. St. Aloysius Gonzaga was known for his love of purity and died at age twenty-two while in the seminary. Many other saints were known to be holy, and they focused on God from their early years: St. Bernadette, St. Thérèse of the Child Jesus, St. Lucy, St. Catherine of Siena and St. Philomena. St. John Berchmans, the patron of altar boys, was twenty-two years old when he died. His three favorite things were his crucifix, his book containing the Rule of his Order and his Rosary.

The most honored of all Saints, Mary the Blessed Virgin, Mother of God, was so open to God's will for her that she said yes to her role in God's plan of salvation when she was a teenager. She had such a good prayer life that she knew the

refused the sexual advances of a teenaged boy who worked on the same farm as her family. When Maria began to resist him, he stabbed her fourteen times. She said she would rather die than sin. As she was dying in the hospital, she told the priest at her side that she would forgive her murderer. Maria was canonized a saint by Pope Pius XII in 1950. She was chosen to be the patron saint of purity for boys and girls.

If Christ could forgive his executioner from the Cross, maybe we should be more patient with people who criticize us for following Him.

Yeah, but do you think that will impress them?

Not necessarily, but maybe they are really searching, and sometimes a little kindness goes a long way.

difference between God's will and her will. She had the grace and the courage to do His will. She may have even had to endure the gossip of her friends and neighbors, who may not have believed that she was pregnant with the Son of God. Even Joseph doubted her until the angel appeared to him in a dream. It was only God's love that sustained her through her difficult days. Mary was one teenager who really said yes to God, and that made a difference for all of us.

St. Joseph, Mary's chaste spouse and the one who had the role of father in the Holy Family, is also a patron for chastity.

Conversions

Some canonized saints and great prophets have shown us that change is possible. St. Augustine and King David had the grace to see that their sins offended God, and hurt themselves and others. They returned to God and experienced His forgiveness and love.

By the grace of God, whole lives can be turned around. In John's Gospel, the woman caught in adultery was about to be stoned to death. Jesus saved her,

and called her to the command of love: "Neither do I condemn you; go, and do not sin again" (John 8:11b). St. Augustine turned away from a life of immorality to become a great Church leader. He realized that true happiness is found in the love of Christ.

Breathe in me,
O Holy Spirit.
Draw me on and
Open wide my heart
to Your love.
Strengthen me,
Guard me,
Guide me.

—St. Augustine

People who love Christ will fight for His triumph. They'll win the battle against sin in themselves and in the world. Some saints start out this way, and others realize only later how much God loves and cares for them. All saints show the joy, happiness and strength that come from knowing Christ and living His way.

In order to put on chastity,
you must put on Christ.

Write a short article in the form of a news report about a saint or someone else who has lived out God's plan for human love. Consider some of the heroes for chastity that Pope John Paul II beatified: Blessed Laura Vicuna, Blessed Teresa Bracco, Blessed Vilmos Apor, Blessed Maria Nangapeta, Blessed Pierina Morasine.

_____

_____

_____

_____

_____

_____

_____

_____

Saints and martyrs notable for chastity (from left to right):

Blessed Kateri Tekakwitha (Mohawk)
Saint Denis Ssebuggwawo (Ugandan)
Saint Joan of Arc (French)
Saint Agatha Kim (Korean)
Saint Dominic Savio (Italian)
Saint Maria Goretti (Italian)

"It is the great multitude of saints—both known and unknown—in whose lives the Lord has opened up the Gospel before us and turned over the pages; he has done this throughout history and he still does today. . . . They show us the way to attain happiness, they show us how to be truly human. . . . Only from the Saints, only from God does true revolution come, the definitive way to change the world."

Pope Benedict XVI, Address at World Youth Day Vigil, August 20, 2005

THE GREAT RACE

What do you remember?

PART I. MATCHING—Put the letter of the correct definition in the blank before each word.

1. _____ conscience
2. _____ free will
3. _____ sin
4. _____ consequences
5. _____ temptation
6. _____ virtues
7. _____ occasion of sin
8. _____ modesty
9. _____ fornicator
10. _____ self-control
11. _____ contraception
12. _____ guilt
13. _____ true sorrow
14. _____ intercession

A. Being sorry for our sins because we love God and are sorry for offending Him

B. The habit of controlling our desires so that we do what we should instead of what we want to do

C. A situation that we know could cause ourselves and others to sin

D. The interior voice that tells us what is the correct moral choice in a given situation

E. The gift given to us by God whereby we can choose how we will think or act

F. The result of our actions, good or bad

G. Prayer to God on someone else's behalf

H. The habits of acting according to what is good and right that make our lives easier and more joyful

I. An offense against God—choosing to go against what we know is right

J. An invitation to sin

K. The virtue by which we guard our senses to protect our purity and the purity of others—an outward sign of our self-respect

L. One who has sexual relations outside of marriage

M. The use of drugs or devices to prevent the conception and birth of a child

N. The result of knowing that you have done something wrong and have not made up for it

PART II. FILL IN THE BLANK OR BLANKS —with the correct words to complete the meaning of the sentence.

God	infatuation	temptation	abusing
modesty	love	control	Ten Commandments
parents	Holy Spirit	thoughts	offend
admit	guilt		

1. The _____ are God's rules that guide and protect us.

2. Christ revealed the Law's meaning by teaching us that _____ is the reason for following the Ten Commandments.

3. When we have grown in love for Christ, we obey not only for the sake of being obedient, but also because we love Christ and do not want to _____ Him.

4. Christ taught us that we are responsible not only for our actions but also for our _____.

5. We should work to form good habits so we can resist the _____ to sin.

6. When we sin, we need to _____ it, ask for forgiveness and work to change our lives.

7. _____ is a "put-on" that protects our senses and guards our purity.

8. Our bodies are temples of the _____.

9. One way to make good decisions is to consider what your _____ would say if they were present, and what _____ thinks—because He is always present.

10. We must be careful not to confuse love with _____.

11. When we sin, by _____ the gifts He gave us, we disturb the order God created.

12. Artificial birth control does not encourage self-_____, which is a necessary step toward maturity.

13. _____ is a natural consequence of sin that should lead us to be sorry for the wrong we have done.

PARENT–TEEN DISCUSSION
Let's Discuss Dating
Discuss these dating questions with your parents:

1. What is a good age to begin:
Group dating _____
Double dating _____
Single dating _____
Steady dating _____
Marriage _____

2. Should dating involve a variety of people or just one special person? Why or why not?

3. Should there be a dating curfew (limit on time to come in)? What is reasonable?

4. Why should teens never drink beer, wine or any other alcohol on a date?

5. What should someone do to avoid and/or resist pressure to do wrong on a date?

6. Honest affection should express the depth of your relationship and not be based only on feelings. What kind of relationship is expressed in each of these forms of affection?
Arms around each other _____
Holding hands _____
Good-night kiss _____
Hugging or cuddling _____
Passionate kissing _____

The corresponding questionnaire for your parents, as well as ideas for discussion, are found in the accompanying *Parent Guide*.

Questions for Further Discussion at Home
- Can teenagers really be in love?
- How do you know when you're in love?
- How do you get a boy or girl to notice you?
- How do you tell the other person that you like him or her?
- How do you ask a girl on a date?
- How do you say no without hurting feelings?
- How can you feel accepted if no one asks you out?
- What do you do on a date?
- Why date?
- If your date does something you don't agree with, what should you do?
- How do you say no to sexual advances?
- How do you break up with someone?

THE CALL TO SERVE CHRIST IN LOVE

Living a life of prayerful chastity for Christ will open the "ears" of our souls so that we can hear His call to serve.

In this unit we will see the many ways that Christ calls us to serve Him. These are the vocations to priesthood, marriage, and consecrated religious life. Each one has its special place in God's plan.

The most important message to remember is that Christ is not asking the impossible of us—He is asking the best of us. Let's serve Him with love, and show His love to the world.

Chapter

Nineteen —LET ME GET THAT CALL

—Following God's plan for chastity leaves us free to discern our proper vocation.

—The celibate life allows people to channel all of their energy into loving God and serving their neighbor.

—We can promote the call to priesthood and consecrated religious life and pray for those who have answered that call already.

—We need to listen for God's call in our own lives.

Chapter

Twenty —TO LOVE AND HONOR . . . TILL DEATH

—Matrimony is a sacrament in which the couple is called to reflect God's love and commitment to each other and to the world.

—The Church teaches that married love should be total, faithful, fruitful and fully human.

—The Sacrament of Matrimony gives dignity to sexual expression.

Chapter

Twenty-One —LOVE AND LIFE: THE HEAVENLY BOND

—The love-life bond was made by God and must not be broken by man.

—God has a fulfilling plan for chaste sexual expression in marriage.

—The Church guides us in living God's plan for sexuality within marriage.

LET ME GET THAT CALL

Freedom to Love

Following God's plan of chastity helps us in discerning our proper vocation. A vocation is a call from God to a particular way of life. Living a chaste and pure life allows us to have the peace of soul necessary to hear the call of Jesus. If we stay in God's graces, develop the virtue of chastity as well as the other virtues, and then **listen** to His word, we will be more able to discover the vocation God has intended for us.

We don't want to "fall into" a vocation or "be stuck" in a life we may later regret. Stay free with chastity. Your happiness could depend on it!

Celibate Love

Our primary purpose in life is to love God and our neighbor as Christ loves us. We can do this whether we are in the married state or the single state.

Many people live celibate lives. They are nuns, priests, religious brothers, some deacons and many single adults who are consecrated to live as Christ in the secular world. They channel all of their energy into loving God and continuing the saving mission of Jesus. If they were not celibate, they would not be able to serve God with the same amount of energy and single-mindedness. Family responsibilities take time and effort that those who are unmarried can give to their work for God. "Jesus has pointed out by work and example the vocation of virginity for the sake of the Kingdom of Heaven. Virginity is a vocation to love; it renders the heart more free to love God" (*Educational Guidance in Human Love*, no. 31).

> To be sure
>
> Be pure.

Priesthood and Consecrated Religious Life

It is important to pray for those who have answered the call to priesthood or consecrated religious life. They have taken vows to imitate Christ more closely. By doing this, they become life partners with Christ. We should thank God that they have said Yes to His call to this holy life. The sacrifices they make are dedicated to the service of Christ's Church, and their sacrifices and prayers help each one of us as members of the Mystical Body.

It is very important to pray for our friends and ourselves so that we will know whom Christ is calling to the priesthood and consecrated life. There is always a need for these vocations. Christ reminds us in the gospel that "The harvest is plentiful but the laborers are few" (Matthew 9:37).

What can we do to promote more vocations to the priesthood and consecrated life?

- Pray for vocations.
- Go to one of the information weekends that are offered by religious orders or your diocesan vocations office.
- Listen carefully for your own call.
- Pray for current priests and religions that they remain faithful to God's call.
- Be kind to priests and members of religious orders, talk to them, help them, invite them over, work with them on parish activities.

It is possible that our involvement in worldly things or activities has kept some of us from hearing God's call. We may not be able to hear His voice amid the noise, modern conveniences, pleasure seeking and selfishness all around us. It is also possible that when we hear His call, we ignore it, dismiss it or just say no!

We can recognize the call of Christ only when we know what His voice sounds like. To keep the lines open, we should always stay in the state of grace with frequent Communion and confession. Communicating with God through prayer is essential. When you are stuck for words, start by saying favorite prayers such as the Our Father, the Hail Mary, the Memorare or the Morning Offering. Or turn off the noise and just listen. Silence gives God and us a chance. Silent reading of a daily Scripture passage and quiet reflection time afterward gives us a chance to listen to God with our hearts.

The Virgin Mary

When Jesus saw his mother, and the disciple whom he loved standing near, he said to his mother, "Woman, behold, your son!" Then he said to the disciple, "Behold, your mother!" And from that hour the disciple took her to his own home.

—John 19:26–27

Mary, the Mother of God, is a great example of pure love. She is human and yet never sinned. She overcame all temptations and was able to do God's will. It was Mary's love for God that made it possible for Jesus Christ to live in her womb for nine months before He was born as both God and man. Her simple acceptance of God's will, "Let it be to me according to your word", is the turning point in human history.

Because of Mary's great holiness, she was chosen to be the Mother of God. Her obedience made up for Eve's disobedience. Just as Eve had led Adam into sin, Mary gave us Christ to lead us out of sin by humbly obeying God's will. In this she became the most blessed of all women, Christ's Mother and our Mother, too.

When we are considering our vocation and God's will for our lives, let us remember to approach Mary as our Mother. Pray for her loving guidance and follow her example. Mary's prayerful purity allowed her to understand clearly and accept lovingly God's will for her.

Mother Mary, help me to be pure.

Another important way to communicate with God is Eucharistic Adoration, when Jesus is exposed in the Blessed Sacrament, and people from the parish come to pray quietly for a holy hour on a regular basis. To develop a friendship with Christ so that you can hear His voice, try spending time with Him as a friend. These are time-tested ways of communicating with God that will help us recognize Christ's voice when He calls.

"Behold, I am the handmaid of the Lord; let it be to me according to your word."

—Luke 1:38

chapter Twenty

TO LOVE AND HONOR . . . TILL DEATH

"Marriage is the wise institution of the Creator to realize in mankind His design of love" (*Humanae Vitae*). It is modeled after the covenant God made with the Jewish nation in the Old Testament to be permanent, faithful and life giving. In the New Testament, marriage has been raised to the level of a sacrament. Matrimony is a visible sign of the bond of love between Christ and His Church. A married couple reflects the love of God.

How Do I Know If It's Love?

Marriage is more than a human partnership: it is an agreement between a man, a woman and **God.** According to the Catholic Church's teaching on marriage in *Humanae Vitae,* married love should have four special qualities:

You mean marriage is a call from God?

Yes, and it makes a difference when people treat it as a vocation, too!

1. Married love should be fully **human.** It must be more than instinct or romance; it should include one's feelings, senses, intellect and spirit. To be fully human, married love must be an act of free will; a choice to give one's life to one's spouse. Based in all the human elements, the couple's love can grow and deepen as they choose to share the joys and sorrows of daily life.
2. Married love must be **total.** The couple must not hold back or remain selfish but should develop a generous friendship. They must not love just because or when their spouse loves them. They must offer themselves completely so their spouse can grow from the gifts they freely share. Marriage is a total self-gift of one to the other.
3. Married love must be **faithful,** exclusive until death. Faithfulness means the spouses guard their hearts from any person, place or thing that could harm their love. This may even include jobs or hobbies that keep us from cherishing our spouse. Faithfulness is not always easy, but it is always good. God would never divorce Himself from us, and because marriage is like God's covenant of love with us, He teaches that divorce from one spouse and remarriage to another is wrong. The example of so many married couples down through the centuries shows us that fidelity agrees with the nature of marriage, and that it is a source of deep and lasting happiness.
4. Married love is **fruitful,** or fertile. It is meant to live on through children, the incarnate love of the couple that lives for all eternity. It doesn't end with the husband and wife but reaches out. It multiplies and gives new life and love to the world, to the Church and to God. Children are God's gift to marriage. It is a privilege to share in the creative power of God. Couples are also challenged to grow in God's love because of the experiences of parenthood. Even if a couple

has not been blessed with their own biological children, they can find many life-giving opportunities, many ways to share their love and make it grow beyond the boundaries of their marriage. Love isn't love until you give it away!

The Sacrament of Love

People who dream of marriage want it to be perfect. And that's not surprising, since God made us with a built-in desire for the best. That's what He wants for us, too—great love and great marriage. This is what we hope for and pray for if God calls us to the vocation of marriage.

In our lives we have already seen many marriages. We look at some and say, "My marriage would never be like that." We see other marriages and think, "That's how I want my marriage and family to be." How can we improve our chances of having a good marriage? The possibility of having a great marriage will be increased if you:

- Become a chaste, mature and virtuous person before marriage.
- Stay close to Christ in prayer as you choose the best person to marry.
- Live according to God's plan of virtuous love during the marriage.

> Love is not a feeling.
> Love is an act of the will.

The success of marriage will include not only some good human skills like listening well and speaking kindly and effectively but also some of the cardinal virtues.

Which of the cardinal virtues is needed to live these aspects of marriage? Prudence, Justice, Fortitude or Temperance?

_____ when to talk, what to say, when to act, and when to be silent

_____ not always getting your own way, and being fair to everyone in the family

_____ never giving up on love and unity, fighting sin from entering your relationship, having courage to raise a Godly family

_____ balance in all things like money, food, health, work, intimacy, emotions, entertainment and use of time

The Gift of Romance

Romantic love is a beautiful gift from God. It is part —yes, only part—of the gift of human and total love. Romantic feelings are good and powerful. They draw us out of ourselves and help us desire to serve another person. These feelings help us to practice unselfish love. Although they are part of love, they are not love. They are an emotional part of love and are good. A person cannot make a lifetime commitment based only on emotions or feelings, though. It is important to know that in total human love, our intellects and wills must be involved. We must use our intellects to help us decide whom to marry or not to marry, or in deciding how to act during marriage. We must use our wills to choose to act in a loving way whether or not we "feel like" loving. In marriage, this is where the graces of the sacrament can help us—strengthening our minds and wills to do good. This is something you don't see on television shows and in movies that equate feelings with love. Even in marriage, romantic feelings can come and go, but the covenant of love is ever present.

As a husband and wife work to become one in their marriage, it's important that they draw upon the graces the sacrament of marriage offers. Many times, they'll need self-sacrifice or forgiveness that seems beyond human limits. Their natural tendencies to be self-centered instead of other-centered might creep into their relationship (remember that original sin?). That's when they need to call upon God's graces offered through the Sacrament of Matrimony, Holy Communion and confession. God's love is limitless. If

117

spouses love each other with God's love, their unity will grow. Their marriage will become a sign of Christ's everlasting union with His Church. In marriage, couples are called to reflect God's love and commitment, and to be His example of His love in the world today. That is the task of all Christian families.

Sacrament of Dignity

When marriage is lived as a sacrament, then it is worthy of the dignity of sexual expression. Sex outside of the sacramental union of marriage is a lie. In fornication, or sex outside of marriage, the body language is saying "I give myself to you", "total gift" and "becoming one", while the mind and will are not. Outside of marriage, sexual expression cannot be fully human, faithful, total or responsible for any fruits of the union. That's why in God's plan:

> Marriage is a permanent,
> total commitment, and true
> sexual union is both life
> giving and love giving.

Let's Discuss the Vows

In the marriage ceremony, there are generally two choices of forms for the spoken vows of consent. Discuss what these mean in light of the sacramental meaning of the marriage covenant.

"I _____ take you _____ to be my (husband/wife). I promise to be true to you in good times and in bad, in sickness and in health. I will love you and honor you all the days of my life."

Our Married Love

Works	Listens
Plays	Prays
Laughs	Forgives
Cries	Lives

"I _____ take you _____ for my lawful wedded (wife/husband), to have and to hold, from this day forward, for better, for worse, for richer, for poorer, in sickness and in health, until death do we part."

Find out which vows were taken by your grandparents; parents; older brothers and sisters.

Ready to See How Love and Life Go Together?

To help us better understand the bond between love and life, try the following experiment before starting the next chapter:

Take two pieces of paper. Write *Love* on one and *Life* on the other. Glue them together back to back, and let them dry overnight.

I have a hunch that love and life cannot be separated without doing some damage.

LOVE AND LIFE: THE HEAVENLY BOND

Remember that there are two purposes for sexual union?

LOVE GIVING—to unite spouses in ever-deepening love by renewing the marriage covenant

LIFE GIVING—to bring children into the world

Fertility, the ability to give life, is a great gift from God. The life-giving property of the marital act is not just an addition to marital love; life-giving naturally comes from giving one's whole self to another person in marriage.

Through the wisdom of the Holy Spirit, our Church teachings on human life are founded on the order of nature created by God:

There is an inseparable connection, *willed by God that is unable to be broken by man on his own*, between the unitive meaning (love-giving) and the procreative meaning (life-giving) of the marital act. While uniting husbands and wives in love, it makes possible the generation of new life. (*Humanae Vitae*, no. 12)

The love-life bond was made by God. We shouldn't try to break it. If we take the life-giving potential out of the marriage act, it loses the fullness of love:

Since we are made in the divine image, our love should mirror God's love. When a man and a woman love and express that love through their sexual powers, they can give life. In fact, if human persons artificially exclude life from the sexual act, they are not expressing love. They are only having sex. There is only one kind of love: the way God loves. Love which is not at least potentially life-giving is not love at all. (from *The Wonder of Human Sexuality* by Fr. Richard Hogan)

Marital Chastity, Naturally Wonderful

God has a fulfilling plan for chaste living in marriage. We have learned that outside of marriage everyone must abstain from sexually pleasurable activities. Within marriage, the virtue of chastity still helps preserve the purity of sexual relations by limiting sexual pleasures to those that are potentially life giving.

Protecting the unity of God's love giving and life giving in marriage includes being open to sharing God's life with children, the natural fruit of marital love, in each act of conjugal love. This does not mean, however, that a couple becomes pregnant with each marital act. God designed our bodies in such a way that we have the ability to be both generous and responsible with our gift of fertility.

A marital life that keeps life and love together glorifies God and also helps married couples grow in:

- Cooperation
- Communication
- Trust
- Generosity

Natural Family Planning

Practicing Natural Family Planning (NFP) is one way couples can answer God's call to protect the love and life bond in their marriage. NFP is a way to cooperate with God in marriage by acting in harmony with the way He created our bodies. God made men fertile all of the time, and He made women fertile for only a few days each month. There are natural, physical signs that show a woman which days she is fertile (able to become pregnant) and which days she is not fertile. NFP provides a system by which a woman may learn to interpret these signs of fertility.

A married couple may then, with thoughtful and prayerful consideration, decide to have marital relations during the fertile time of the month, in order to conceive a child with the help of God. If a married couple has serious reasons for avoiding conception at that time, they may choose to abstain from marital relations during the fertile time of that month. NFP is a method of family planning that cooperates with God and nature and respects the love-life bond.

Artificial Birth Control Offends God

Contraception, or artificial birth control, is any attempt at preventing the conception of life in the marriage act. Contraceptive methods can be temporary or permanent (as in sterilization). Contraception is a sin against God and His plan for human love. As with any serious sin, the couple experiences a loss of grace, so the unitive love-giving dimension of their marriage becomes more difficult. It separates a couple that God has joined together in matrimony by breaking the love-life bond. It offends the dignity of the husband and wife who are made in the image of God to reflect His love.

Contraception also offends the goodness of the couple's relationship. Couples who are totally giving of themselves want nothing between them. When a man and a woman totally love one another, they love the whole person which includes fertility.

We should be grateful that the Church upholds this teaching against contraception. This truth will protect married love. The divorce statistics during the four decades after the birth control pill became popular have proven Church teaching to be true. Couples who used contraception had a 50 percent divorce rate. Couples who used Natural Family Planning had only a 4 percent divorce rate. This is not a typing error; this is a huge difference. This is the difference that the grace of God can make. His plan works.

Technological Reproduction

Besides contraception, there is an opposite offense—when people try to remove the love from the love-life bond. Many doctors and scientists try to take the place of God by attempting to separate the power to give life from the personal act of love in marriage.

This offense against God's plan for love and life is done by making babies in laboratories, either by conceiving new lives with their parents' reproductive cells, or by cloning.

The clear teaching of the Church of keeping love and life together is a reflection of God's truth: all children deserve to be conceived by the loving act of a husband and wife. This truth is not based on popularity or public opinion, but rooted in the way God made us. Of course, God loves each and every child who is conceived, even if it is conceived immorally; but, the Church must protect us from using immoral means, even to reach an end that is good. New life is always good, but it will not be respected when it is seen as the product of science or technology. Even now human embryos conceived in laboratories are treated as mere things that can be experimented upon or used for harvesting organs or discarded according to the whims of their makers.

Although married couples do suffer if they are unable to have children on their own, the teaching of the Church in the Vatican document *Donum Vitae* can help them understand how and why all Christians must protect the dignity of the human person. Having children is not a right—it is a gift, a gift from God. A child is not to be used as a piece of property. A woman's body is not to be used as a machine.

This does not necessarily mean that couples who cannot have children right away should not seek medical help. Many new scientific discoveries that are also moral are being developed to help couples who have difficulty conceiving. Institutes of Catholic doctors and scientists are continuously working to solve some of the problems of life giving without offending God and His plan for married couples.

There are other sexual sins that destroy the dignity of human sexuality by breaking the love and life bond. One of these sins is masturbation, which is a way of seeking sexual pleasure for oneself alone. It involves no love giving, and it has no life-giving possibilities. Another is homosexual activity, which has no possibility of life giving and involves no real union, since two people of the same sex were not made to complement one another physically. It is sinful to participate in any act that uses oneself or other persons as objects for sexual pleasure while intentionally avoiding the life-giving and love-giving act of marital sexual intercourse. Pornography is another way that human sexuality is degraded, in which women and men are used as objects, with neither love giving *nor* life giving involved. These are sins because they misuse the sexual powers that God gave us for love and life. If you have any questions about these topics, please ask your parents.

The Love and Life Bond

Now get the *Love* and *Life* papers that you glued together at the end of the last chapter. Try your best to separate the whole *Love* page from the *Life* page. Start at the top and try to tear them apart. What happens? The effort to separate one from the other usually ruins both. The pages cannot be separated without taking away some of the *Life* or some of the *Love* or some of both. And it works that way in real life. Any effort to separate love from life always ends up with a mess!

People who offend God by rejecting His plan cut themselves off from His grace. Every human task then becomes more difficult. People often are deceived into thinking that rejecting parts of God's plan has actually made their lives easier. Satan tricked Eve this way, remember? And Satan has tricked some people into rejecting God's plan for love. The Father of Lies might tell you, "It's not really wrong", "It's not really sex", "It's not really important", "It's not hurting anyone," or "Everything is acceptable if you think you have a reason for it." But falling for these lies does not make our lives easier or happier.

Don't let yourself be fooled. Please don't believe the lies of a culture that does not follow God's commandments. Find your confidence and comfort in the Church that was founded by

Jesus Christ. We are truly blessed to have a Church that will guide us to see the difference between good and evil, use and abuse. Only God delivers true happiness—when we live according to His plan.

Our fertility is an awesome gift. We can use our sexual powers in accordance with God's design, or we can abuse them and do harm to ourselves and to others.

A married couple can make good and wise decisions about their fertility, or infertility as the case may be, when they are close to God through prayer, when they have mutual respect for each other, when they are growing in virtue, and when they seek to know and understand the teachings of the Church and the will of God for their family.

Children are the greatest fruit and blessing of married love. They bring tremendous joy to their parents, but they also bring great responsibilities.

God's plan for married love allows couples to embrace all the joy as well as anticipate and fulfill all of the responsibilities of family life. To spouses who accept His will and rely on Him for the grace they need to carry it out, He gives all that is needed to love and be loved, to find true happiness in this life and in the life to come.

God's plan helps us to be loved totally and helps us further His Kingdom here on earth.

*Do not think that
God's delays are
God's denials.*

*True Prayer always
receives what it asks—
or something better.*

GOD IS PRO-LIFE AND PRO-LOVE

The Call to Respect Life

Do we ever stop to think about what a wonderful gift life is? God didn't have to create the human race, after all. He gave us life because He loved us. We have nothing that is more precious than life and the love that gives it meaning and purpose.

God has loved each person who has ever lived. He loves us all. And He wants everyone to have a chance to enjoy the life He gives.

We know from earlier chapters of this book that God also showed us His love by creating us in His own image. We have great dignity because we are made in His likeness. Another way God showed how special humans are was to send us Jesus, in human flesh, to die for us. Think of it! Each of us is so valuable to God that, even if you were the only person who had ever lived, Jesus would have died for you.

Life Begins at Conception

God loves each person from the very beginning of life, from the moment of conception.

Several Scripture verses show us that our dignity and value as human beings begin even before we are born. Look up the following passages and explain how they show that we are called to respect human life.

> Jeremiah 1:5
> Psalm 139:13–16
> Luke 1:5–38
> Luke 1:39–56

Now we can better understand why abortion, the killing of an unborn baby, is wrong. People use many excuses for abortion. After all, in our culture all kinds of things are disposable. We're taught that when we finish something or get tired of it we can

throw it away. If we need it again we can always buy another one. Unfortunately, many people have begun to think that human life is disposable, too. They think that if caring for a new baby would be inconvenient or cause them some suffering, then it is okay to kill the baby. It's a tragedy that unborn babies, if they are less than perfect or are inconvenient, are simply destroyed. God has a unique plan for every person ever conceived. It's not our place to decide who should have the chance to fulfill God's plan and who should not.

Life is always a gift of God's love. God is always present for life to be given because He creates an immortal soul. God gives life and takes it away. These are events in which we should not interfere.

If a child is conceived outside of marriage, some people may erroneously think that they can get rid of the "mistake". But we know that God never makes a mistake. When a child is conceived by an unmarried couple, or even by a horrible sin like rape or incest, God's love is still present in that baby.

Why should the child be condemned to death for its parent's sin? What an injustice is such a death! Peace and justice cannot thrive in a world that sees killing innocent babies as an answer to its problems. One sin is not erased by compounding it with another. Our merciful Father forgives sin, and we should turn to God when we need help carrying our burdens.

Abortion Is Always Wrong

Look up and write the main points from the following quotes from the *Catechism* regarding abortion: Part Three, Life in Christ; Article 5, the Fifth Commandment.

1. Read paragraph 2258 and explain why human life is sacred. _____

_____

_____

2. Read paragraph 2268 and explain what the fifth commandment forbids. _____

_____

_____

3. Read paragraph 2270 and explain when the human right to life begins. _____

_____

_____

4. Read paragraph 2271 and document the history of Christian teaching against abortion. _____

_____

_____

5. Read paragraph 2272 and explain the canonical penalty incurred by a person who procures an abortion. _____

_____

_____

6. Read paragraph 2273 and explain why so many pro-life organizations are answering God's call to change the laws that allow abortion.

_____

_____

7. Read article 2275 and explain why producing embryos for experimentation is wrong.

_____

_____

8. Explain how chastity can eliminate the popularity of abortion. _____

_____

_____

God's Mercy

We need to pray that abortion, a crime against innocent lives, will stop. But we also need to help those who have had abortions to know that they can be forgiven. Otherwise, their guilt from committing such a serious sin may cripple them. They need to find the peace and healing that only Jesus can offer. They need to know that God still loves them and wants to give them a fresh start.

You Can Help the Cause of Life!
Find out what pro-life organizations you have in your area. What do they do? How do they help unwed mothers? Babies? Do they help counsel women who already had an abortion and are suffering in their hearts? Do they help change the laws that allow abortion? Do they have a teen pro-life group? Do they need teen volunteers?

Dear God,
There is a sad young woman out there today
Who's heard some news she'd rather not say,
She thinks it's a secret—that baby inside,
And, Lord, she wants to run and hide.
She feels ashamed she's done some wrong,
She can't face the world, 'cause she's not strong.

O God of compassion, please be her guide,
And Jesus—you suffered—stay at her side.
Send someone to tell her that life is good
And the baby deserves to get the care it should.
You've got to send someone to show her your love.
Can't You come down from those skies above?
What's that? You want me to? But what can I do?
I'd better think fast before that baby is through.

I'll help her and love her and say her baby's good
so she'll respect life the way that she should.
Give me strength, Lord.
Amen.

Our heroes today should be those who fight abortion and help women with unwanted pregnancies. Christ provides loving answers through His people, so there is never a need to kill an unborn baby. If you know someone who is troubled by a pregnancy, she may be feeling lost, helpless, rejected or angry. She needs love and friendship to help her through this time. In addition to reaching out to her yourself, check your phone book or ask your priest about local pro-life organizations. These, too, are sources of friendship and help to pregnant women.

The Adoption Option

Some unmarried parents may recognize that they are not yet ready for the responsibility of raising a child. A morally good choice for them is to place the child for adoption. Adoption gives childless couples the chance to experience the joys of parenthood. It gives the child the chance to be raised in a home that has both a mother and a father to provide care and guidance. Unlike abortion, adoption is a life-giving and selfless choice.

DO IT FOR GOD; HE'S DONE IT FOR YOU

What an awesome God! His plan for life and love is so beautiful. So simple and yet so profound. Not even a human genius could have thought up this one!

In His wisdom He has let us know that chastity is possible, good and livable. In His mercy He continues to call us to His plan. In His love he continues to give us His life!

So the challenge is on: to be a Christian in today's world and to obey the law of love whether or not it's popular.

GROW IN HIS LOVE
KNOW HIS WILL
CHOOSE TO LIVE IT

The accomplishment of that holy will is not always easy, but it was not so even for Jesus. However difficult it is, we may be sure it is far less difficult than the frustration of choosing any other will. The choice of evil over good is always more painful in the end than the momentary pain of self-control.

We were created from love and we love in order to live. We are out of place and things just don't seem to fit right when we try to be anything else than what we were created to be—good, loving, joyful, compassionate, kind, understanding, chaste and holy, "holy as our Heavenly Father is holy."

—Mother Angelica

Accepting the Challenge

Teens are up to the challenge. They have the energy, enthusiasm and grace to strive for real love. The following pointers can help any person, young or old, achieve the true love the human heart desires.

1. Remember the first commandment and make God number one in your life. Let nothing come between your love for Him and His love for you.

2. Pray often. Make Jesus your most dependable Friend by telling him all that is in your mind and heart. He always listens, and He always answers.

3. Receive the sacraments of Penance and Communion frequently. There is no substitute for supernatural grace.

4. Listen to the Church. She is a good mother and a faithful teacher; her moral guidance is trustworthy.

5. Listen to those in authority over you—parents, priests and teachers who are trying to steer you toward truth and goodness deserve your respect and obedience.

> From frequent and intimate contact with the Lord, young people will derive the strength and enthusiasm for a pure life and they will realize their human and Christian vocation in peaceful self-control and in generous giving to others.
>
> —E. G. H. Love

> Act as if everything depended on you, and pray as if everything depended on God.

6. Develop a positive and grateful attitude. Count your blessings every day and thank God for them. Do not listen to the voices that try to tear you down and make you feel sorry for yourself.

7. Make friends with people who share your faith, who respect you, and who value the virtue of chastity.

8. Be generous with your time, energy and talent. It is in giving of ourselves that we find our happiness. Do good works at home, school and church.

9. Practice the virtue of self-control in all things – talking, eating, studying, sleeping, doing chores and exercising or participating in organized sports. If we do not practice disciplining ourselves, we will have a difficult time being chaste.

10. Stay pure in thoughts, words and deeds. Be modest in dress. Take responsibility for what you see, hear and think. With courage resist the negative influences around you that seek to cheapen human life and love.

Showing What You Know

You have learned a great deal about embracing God's plan for love and life — what it is, why it is desirable, and how to put into practice. Read the following actions and explain how they can help you fulfill God's plan for your happiness.

PRACTICE	WHY THIS IS A GOOD PRACTICE
1. Asking my parents, rather than my friends, the questions I have about sexuality.	
2. Finding out what the Church really teaches about sex from credible sources.	
3. Going to Mass and confession regularly.	
4. Praying daily.	
5. Praying for God to reveal my vocation — whether marriage, priesthood, or consecrated religious life.	
6. Postponing serious, one-on-one dating until I am ready for marriage.	
7. Dressing modestly.	
8. Refusing to tell or listen to stories or jokes that disrespect sexuality.	
9. Practicing self-control in all areas of my life.	
10. Avoiding sexually suggestive books, movies, magazines and music.	
11. Making friends with people who share my faith and values.	
12. Planning activities that will promote, not discourage, my Christian growth.	

CALL TO SERVE CHRIST IN LOVE
What Do You Remember?

PART I. MATCHING—Put the letter of the correct definition in the blank before the correct word.

1. _____ vocation
2. _____ virginity
3. _____ Matrimony
4. _____ commitment
5. _____ abortion

6. _____ adoption
7. _____ *Humanae Vitae*
8. _____ marital chastity
9. _____ pro-life organizations
10. _____ consecrated religious life

A. A promise to carry out a responsibility.
B. Faithfulness to spouse and openness to life; protects the love-giving and life-giving bond
C. A call from God to a particular state in life
D. The sacrament by which a man and a woman become one flesh in a bond resembling the one between Christ and His Church
E. The papal letter that confirmed the Church's continuous teaching against artificial birth control and instructed us on the bond of love and life in marriage
F. The killing of an unborn child
G. A state of life in which a person takes the vows of poverty, chastity and obedience
H. The process by which a couple unable to properly care for their child place him in a good home
I. Source of friendship and help to pregnant women
J. A state of life that "renders the heart more free to love God", not having engaged in a physical sexual relationship

PART II. FILL IN THE BLANK OR BLANKS—with the correct word or phrase to complete the meaning of the sentence. Some words will be used more than once.

livable	baby	love
conception	Natural Family Planning (NFP)	free
sin	God	virginity
graces	technological reproduction	life

1. Marriage is an agreement between the couple and

_____.

2. _____ is a way to work with God and nature to space children.

3. Following God's plan of chastity leaves us _____ to hear God's call.

4. Some people are called to the chaste celibate life, meaning they are unmarried and committed to singleheartedly serving _____ for the rest of their lives.

5. The Sacrament of Matrimony provides the husband and wife with the power to grow in love for each other by relying on the _____ of God.

6. The marital act must be _____ giving and _____ giving.

7. Life begins at _____.

8. Abortion, a serious sin, is the killing of an unborn _____.

9. One _____ is not erased by compounding it with another.

10. Chastity is possible, good and _____.

11. _____ disrupts God's plan for a child to be conceived within the loving act of his parents.

PARENT–TEEN DISCUSSION

- What are we doing in our family to encourage religious vocations?
- Do we express any attitudes that discourage religious vocations?
- What advantages are there to chastity?
- What can we do in our family that will help our teens hear their vocation?
- What would you look for in a marriage partner?
- Why are sacramental graces needed for marriage?
- What are some serious reasons for spacing children in marriage?
- What method for spacing children has been approved by the Church?
- How can the attitudes of our family prevent abortion?
- What can we do in our family to support and encourage chaste living?

chapter Twenty-Four

TAKE THE PLEDGE FOR PURITY

One of the biggest decisions you will ever make is how, when and to whom you give the astonishing gift of yourself.

The lies of the world disguise the real choices. You can choose to live love to the fullest in all its mystery; or you can steal glimpses of its pleasures, alienating yourself from the One Who is Love and corrupting the greatest possibilities of this gift.

Chastity pays off now with the deep joy that comes only from doing God's will. Chastity pays off now with grace and union with God. Chastity pays off now with an opportunity to develop better-quality friendships. Chastity helps you to avoid or break the habits of thought, word or action that cripple your capacity to love.

Chastity is much more than abstinence, although abstinence is part of chastity. Chastity includes sexual abstinence, which means abstaining from sexually arousing thoughts, words and actions. Yet, chastity is a virtue that brings you the freedom to love others with the affection of Christ. Chastity frees you to love Christ and to better know His will for you and for your relationships.

Making a firm decision to practice chastity can bring you into adulthood with deeper happiness and greater freedom. Removing sexually pleasurable activities from the dating scene and keeping them where they belong—in marriage—frees you to grow in virtue, instead of fighting for your virtue during your dating years.

Christians who practice chastity don't have to worry about or plan "what moves to make". They can concentrate instead on developing good friendships with people who are made in the image of God. A chaste person has more freedom to hear God's call to a religious vocation or to wisely choose a marriage partner. A person can reap the many benefits of staying close to God in prayer and desiring a clean heart.

Since chastity protects love from the perils of selfishness and aggressiveness, a reputation for being chaste may keep selfish and aggressive people from even wanting to date us. What a blessing!

There is something very human about making a promise out loud in front of other people. There is something in our conscience that makes us want to keep our promises. It is a social commitment, as well as a personal one, that makes us accountable to others who expect the best of us. So, now that we have learned the importance of purity and chastity, it's time to take the pledge.

Take this pledge for purity, and experience the freedom of the virtue of chastity!

The Challenge to Be Pure in Thoughts, Words and Actions

In order to honor God, respect myself and affirm the dignity of love and life:

I promise to practice chastity from now on, and in the future vocation to which God calls me.

Signature_____ Date_____

Upon completion of the *Love and Life* program, witnessed by_____

(parent or teacher)
